FUNDRAISING IDEAS

FUNDRAISING IDEAS

*Over 225 Money Making Events
for Community Groups,
with a Resource Directory*

by
JANELL SHRIDE AMOS

Illustrations by STEPHEN WAYNE HOFFMAN

McFarland & Company, Inc., Publishers
Jefferson, North Carolina, and London

This book is dedicated to my sister, Peggy Shride Hart,
in honor of all we share—our heritage,
the memories, the good times and the bad times

British Library Cataloguing-in-Publication data are available

Library of Congress Cataloguing-in-Publication Data

Amos, Janell Shride, 1938–
    Fundraising ideas : over 225 money making events for community
groups, with a resource directory / by Janell Shride Amos.
        p.   cm.
    Includes bibliographical references and index.
    ISBN 0-7864-0072-2 (sewn softcover : 55# alk. paper) ∞
    1. Fund raising—United States—Handbooks, manuals, etc.   2. Fund
raising—United States—Directories.   I. Title.
HV41.9.U5A45   1995
361.7'068'1—dc20   95-16638
                                                             CIP

Manufactured in the United States of America

McFarland & Company, Inc., Publishers
  Box 611, Jefferson, North Carolina 28640

ACKNOWLEDGMENTS

Individuals who serve as volunteers to help raise funds for worthy causes are very special; many graciously shared their experiences and ideas with me. With gratitude I acknowledge their contributions to the content of this book.

My husband, David, provided valued proofreading services and much patience and support as I worked on this project. Chris and Kim Amos reviewed the manuscript and made suggestions for its improvement. Stephen Hoffman was both creative and efficient as he produced the drawings; it was a pleasure to work with him.

CONTENTS

Contents

PREFACE

This book contains programs which can be used by individuals or organizations to raise money to support a specific worthy cause through special events. The ideas involve various combinations of materials, goods, services and help from professionals, but the main ingredients are the enthusiasm and the labor of volunteers. Methods of obtaining donations by personal or mail solicitation are not addressed.

Sometimes the most difficult part of raising money is the planning and organization stage. The Introduction of the book provides suggestions and guidelines to assist with this phase of a project. "Choosing the Right Fundraisers" presents a process for selecting an appropriate fundraising project. "Making the Basic Decisions" outlines desirable characteristics for key leaders and discusses the basic decisions which must be made by fundraising planners. The importance of planning is stressed in "Planning the Event" and an overview of a desirable committee structure is presented. "Providing the Extras" describes activities and services which, while not contributing directly to profit for a fundraiser, can improve the atmosphere of the event, its attendance, or the enjoyment of those who participate.

Individuals who accept leadership positions for an event or committee will find helpful information in "Organizing the Work," "Promoting Effectively," "Managing the Money," "Honoring the Law," "Dealing with Problems," and "Concluding Activities." Benefits from fundraising events include more than money; some of these are summarized in "Valuing Non-Monetary Benefits."

The largest section of this book contains descriptions of over 225 ideas for raising funds. Ideas for fundraising events are far too numerous to be presented in one book; to consider all the variations and combinations overwhelms the mind. Each event described herein is unique and reflects the needs, talents, and resources of those doing the planning and the characteristics of their supporters and patrons. The idea descriptions are designed to provide inspiration and information for fundraisers; common sense and energy must be applied to tailor the ideas and make them practical and profitable for a particular group.

The idea descriptions, which are arranged in alphabetical order from A-Thons to Yard Booth, include overall project themes and numerous ideas which can be used either alone or as a booth at a larger event. The traditional, tried and proven events are described, but there are also innovative ideas. There are fundraisers that are appropriate for young children with adult helpers and others that are especially appropriate for teenagers or senior citizens. Some of the ideas require many workers; for others only a few are required for success. Likewise the descriptions include ways to make money which require various amounts of capital investment. Few will review the ideas presented and not find several appropriate for their circumstances and group.

Experienced and successful fundraisers were a significant resource in the research done for this book. Success stories are presented for 22 successful fundraising projects and fundraisers. These profiles of success illustrate how an idea is the beginning point for planning an event tailored to the resources and needs of the group needing money. The fundraisers generously share information and suggestions to assist those interested in planning similar projects.

A resource directory is provided to supplement readers' local resources of specialized information and materials. The directory provides names, addresses, phone numbers, and product descriptions. Resources are abundant and no attempt was made to list all possibilities; instead the directory includes selected materials representing a wide variety of possible needs.

Fundraising Ideas is designed to be a basic reference for groups of all kinds that need ideas and assistance in planning projects which will earn money for their cause.

INTRODUCTION

Choosing the Right Fundraisers

With the hundreds of possibilities, how do you decide which fundraiser is best for your group?

There is no single best fundraiser for a group; too many circumstances influence the success of an effort to raise money through a special event. Sometimes one person or a small group has an idea for how the group can raise funds and "sells" that project to the group. More often a group has a need for money and begins the search for one or more fundraising activities. The following suggestions represent one process for choosing a special event to earn money for a worthy cause.

Goal Statement: A leader or a committee prepares a goal statement. The statement indicates in concise terms the amount of money needed, how the money will be used, and a target date for raising the money.

Research Possible Projects: Identify several projects that will be of interest to most members of the group. For each project being considered, answer the following questions:

- How much money can we expect this event to raise?
- Will our potential patrons support this type of event?
- Do we have available the volunteer workers needed?
- Do we have the resources (leadership, up-front money, suitable site, expertise, etc.) needed?
- Is the timing right for our group to do this project?
- Is this an efficient way to earn the money we need?
- Could this event become a new tradition for our group and allow us to benefit from our work and experience by having similar events in the future?

Presentation at General Meeting: Invite all members to a meeting and

1

present the projects which have been researched. Hold an open discussion. Allow the members to suggest other possible events. Consider all concerns and suggestions or adaptations. If possible, adopt one or more projects and set a tentative date.

If you reach a decision on a special event to raise funds, you are ready to begin making basic decisions. Keep in mind the importance and worth of the work you are doing and you will be able to meet all the challenges ahead.

Making the Basic Decisions

The Chairperson and Planning Committee

The first key decision is the appointment of a chairperson. The chairperson will take the lead in making the other basic decisions which should be presented to the leaders of the organization for their approval.

The ideal chairperson might be described as follows:

- is highly motivated and energetic
- is able to enlist other workers
- works well with individuals and groups
- is able to transform ideas into reality
- resolves problems efficiently
- is organized and good with details
- has a good sense of humor
- is calm and cheerful under pressure

If you do not have available a person with all of these characteristics who is willing to serve as chairperson, don't despair. The chairperson can enlist assistants and key committee leaders to compensate for any weak leadership areas. The most important task of the chairperson is to coordinate all activities associated with the fundraiser and keep the team of workers running smoothly.

The basic decisions which must be made by the chairperson and the planning committee are date and hours, location, price, name of event and unifying theme. Some of these decisions may be obvious or already set by the organization. Indicated below are some factors to consider in making these decisions or reviewing predetermined decisions.

Date and Hours

Sometimes it is difficult to determine the best time for a money raising event. Consider the factors which affect the members of the community. Will the children be in school? Are people on vacations? Will the date place you in competition with another conflicting community activity or fundraiser? Is the date compatible with the type of event? If you are selling merchandise, will the date be influenced by buying habits? Can your fundraiser benefit from being held in conjunction with another event already scheduled by your organization or another group?

Most disadvantages that may be associated with a particular date can be overcome with enough promotion and publicity and the production of a quality event. However, it is wise to be alert to the possible problems which need to be overcome.

Location

The site selected should, in general, be convenient for the patrons, be an appropriate size for the event, be comfortable for the participants, offer toilet facilities, and have adequate parking space. If the event is planned for outside, you need an alternate plan for bad weather.

Selecting an unconventional facility enhances some fundraisers. A reception backstage at a theater, lunch in a museum, brunch at a members-only club, dinner on a train, and a reception in a garden spot are examples of ways to make an event more appealing.

Price

Deciding the price to charge for admission, services, merchandise, etc. requires careful thought. The goal is to make as much profit as possible and still be able to attract a crowd or sell the merchandise. If you know of others who have had a profitable fundraiser similar to yours, their prices might be discussed. The best advice is probably to make it a group decision. Whatever price is set, some will think it is too high and some will consider it too low. The wisdom of the decisions can only be judged by the results.

Name and Theme

An attention-attracting title is an asset as long as it is appropriate for the event. A theme can provide a clear focus and influence elements such as the color scheme, the decorations, the entertainment, and the possible costumes of workers during the event.

Planning the Event

Planning is a continuation of preparing for the fundraiser based upon the basic decisions which have been made. This stage will probably broaden

the group of workers making the decisions.

The planners can brainstorm to decide which tasks will influence the success of the event. The resulting list of tasks will provide a basis for establishing committees with designated areas of responsibility. Each major committee will need a chairperson to serve as the leader and coordinator. Be sure the committees include qualified individuals to manage the money, to be sure the group is in compliance with local, state and federal laws, and to coordinate all promotion efforts.

The entire planning team may want to visit the location and inspect the facilities in relation to their tasks. Each group will need to develop a realistic budget for expenses prior to the event. This budget will reflect the group's dedication to the universal rule of fundraisers in relation to items they need: *Get it free. If you can't get it free, get it at cost. If you can't get it at cost, get it wholesale.*

Three overall guidelines have been suggested for those planning fundraising events.

- Strive for quality in every area.
- Be bold and dramatic in the scope of your planning, in the promotions, and in the decorations.
- Make the preparations and event fun for the workers and for those who participate.

There is no substitute for planning!

Providing the "Extras"

Activities and services which do not contribute directly to the profit for a fundraiser can improve the atmosphere of the event, attendance, or the enjoyment of the patrons. Consider providing the following "extras" if you have the resources and they are appropriate for the event:

Costumes. Costumes which support the theme can be worn by workers. Those who attend can be encouraged to dress in costume by having a costume contest with awards given for the best, the most unique, etc.

Door Prizes. Give door prizes which can be won by registering and having your name drawn. Specify whether the person must be present to win. (Include addresses on the registration forms and collect information for creating a mailing list of participants.)

Entertainment. Schedule free entertainment at designated locations or roving the area of the event. The idea is to have volunteers providing entertainment. If costumes are not in order for all workers, perhaps they can be used by the entertainers to support their music or the theme.

Something for the Children. Offer a special attraction for the children to attract families. The attraction could be a carousel, a puppet show, a magician, a roving clown, Santa or the Easter Bunny, a ride on a fire engine, animals to pet, free helium balloons or a make and take art center. Child care may be desirable for some fundraisers.

Refreshments. In some cases inexpensive food or drink can be provided without charge.

Checking Station. Provide a checking service for coats or packages near the entrance.

Shuttle Bus. If parking is at a premium, provide a shuttle bus from parking in another location. A shuttle bus is an appreciated "extra" for events like a house tour or a progressive dinner which require the customers to move from place to place.

Honoring Individuals. Consider honoring a deserving and popular individual at the event. This is especially appropriate for a luncheon, dinner or other fundraiser which features a meal.

Organizing the Work

One of the most difficult and important jobs of the chairperson is finding the best people for each job. Most fundraisers recognize the truth of the principle that raising money is a team sport, but in actual practice, the work is often done by too few people.

Don't expect all of the workers you need to volunteer. Most of the time you must ask someone to do the jobs. Taking a skills survey of the members of your group will make this task easier. Prepare a simple questionnaire that members can fill out at a meeting. The questionnaire should request their name, address, telephone number, business telephone, professional experiences and hobbies and special interests. Have a list for jobs which will need to be done for the fundraiser and have them check the ones they can do. Provide a place for them to list businesses and individuals who might provide goods or services needed for the fundraiser. Don't forget to provide a place for comments.

Distribute flyers to all members telling about the special fundraising event and provide names and telephone numbers which can be called to volunteer to work or offer helpful suggestions. Involve as many members of the group as possible! An important tool for enlisting workers is an up-to-date membership list which gives names, addresses, and telephone numbers. Ask enlisted workers to bring family members and friends to help also.

If the plan is to make the fundraiser an annual event, try to have an intern assist each committee chairperson. This policy will train leadership for the future.

Have each committee develop a definite plan of action which includes a target date for accomplishing each task. The general chairperson should review all the plans to spot any duplications, problems, and opportunities to combine purchases or efforts. A master plan can be constructed which indicates target dates of interest to all committees.

Some businesses like to underwrite entire special events as part of their advertising budget. Others will donate items needed by the fundraisers. A company may buy a block of tickets for its employees. It is difficult to predict the reaction of any businessperson to a request for support. In general the following guidelines should be followed:

- A request for support be made in person by a member of the group; the second choice for contact is a well written letter.
- If possible, contact the individual who has the authority to make a decision.
- Stress the benefits in advertising and goodwill which the business will receive as a result of its support. (Be sure you actually deliver more than you promise in the way of recognition.)

The leaders in charge of the special event must stay in constant touch with every worker, either through the chairperson of the committee or directly. Regular reporting and exchange of information are important. Develop a list of all individuals expected to work before, during and after the special event. Call all the workers to confirm that they can be present, what job they will be doing, and what time they are expected to work. (Be prepared to find replacements for some.) Inform all workers where they can check in and what means will be used to identify the staff for the event. (Badges, arm bands, costume items, etc. are possibilities. Often the theme will suggest a fitting method.)

If appropriate for the event you are planning, prepare a layout of the site indicating where everything will be located. Prepare large, easy-to-read signs to direct the customers. When all preparations are made, walk through the site to see that everything is in order. Stress to everyone your resolve to begin the event on time and end on time.

Promoting Effectively

Choose one person to coordinate all publicity and promotion. That person and his or her committee should start with a plan—which may be as simple as a list of ways to promote the special event and of who will be responsible for taking care of each method.

It is good to have a concise statement which identifies the group which is promoting the special event and states why the financial support is needed and how much money is needed for the cause. This statement will help the members of the group explain to potential workers, supporters, and patrons the reason for raising funds.

Advertise early and frequently, and use a variety of methods. The messages about the event should all include information about who, what, why, where and when. The following list indicates some of the ways a special fundraising event can be promoted:

- Arrange television and radio public service announcements, purchased advertising and feature interviews.
- Secure articles and announcements in community newspapers.
- Display advertising posters, flyers, banners, window signs, and yard signs—the more the better.
- Hand out flyers on street corners and at busy shopping centers, and put them on cars in parking lots.
- Ask local banks and other businesses to enclose a flyer in their mailings and billings.
- Publicize the event by distributing buttons, bumper stickers, pencils or balloons.
- Request advertisement in organization newsletters and church bulletins.
- Encourage the group members to request permission to announce the fundraiser at every meeting they attend.

After the event, send a success story about the fundraiser to the local newspapers and radio and television stations. Send photographs to newspapers with your story. Identify the individuals in the pictures and include a form signed by those in the pictures and the photographer giving permission to print the photographs.

Promotion of a fundraiser cannot be taken lightly; it always affects the success of the event.

Managing the Money

One person should be designated to be in charge of all monetary matters related to the fundraiser. This person and a small committee can serve as the finance committee.

The finance committee has the following responsibilities:

- Establish a budget for pre-event expenses.
- Collect and keep secure all funds received.
- Pay all receipted bills approved by the general chairperson.
- Prepare a written, detailed report of all monetary transactions related to the special event.

In some instances a group may want to have a policy of giving receipts to customers. If the receipt included the purchaser's name and address, keeping a copy for the organization would create a mailing list of supporters for the next fundraiser. Organizing these receipts could be a service provided by the finance committee.

Honoring the Law

Seek advice from a lawyer to assist you in observing all applicable local, state and federal laws. Depending on the type of special event you are conducting, you may need to consider the following:

- Tax laws governing food sales, entertainment, or raffles and games of chance may affect your plans.
- Building, fire and safety regulations will probably apply to your site.
- Health authorities will be concerned with how food is prepared and served.
- Contracts need to be carefully reviewed before they are signed.
- The police department should be informed of the plans for the event; follow their suggestions and accept any assistance they offer.
- Local ordinances will affect serving liquor.
- In some cases you may want to have a security force to protect against theft or disturbances.

Needless to say, it is critically important to keep everything legal.

Dealing with Problems

Most planners of a special fundraising event have problems they did not or could not anticipate. They are what keep things interesting and challenge the leaders' creativity and sanity. There are several precautions, developed to deal with problems experienced by other fundraisers, that the group should take before and during the event.

Designate one or two people to run errands to solve problems. They may need to go purchase an item, pick up the guest speaker with a flat tire, transport an ill person home, or do some other unexpected chore. These people need their cars in reserved parking spots at convenient locations.

Post by the telephones emergency numbers for the police and fire departments and have available telephone numbers for reaching key participants like guest speakers and entertainers.

Be sure the electrical outlets work and know the location of fuse boxes or circuit breakers. Bring extra fuses. Check that the sound system works early in the planning period and up until the last minute. Have backup parking arrangements in case you are blessed with an overflow crowd. If money is changing hands, be sure to prepare cash boxes with the needed supply of money to make change.

Have a representative talk to the neighbors where the event will be held and assure them that those in charge are sensitive to the inconveniences they may have. Tell the neighbors how to reach the representative during the event if they have problems. (At the least, the representative can apologize on behalf of the organization.)

If something is being sold, be sure to have enough bags for packaging. Brief all workers on potential problems and give them guidelines for how they should be handled. (For example, unhappy or obnoxious shoppers may be referred to a designated person.) Designate two or three workers to be "trouble shooters" to move around the site to assist with problems and help where needed. Finally, make a written record of all the unexpected problems so, hopefully, they can be avoided in the future.

Concluding Activities

After the fundraising event there are still a number of tasks to be completed. The first is to clean up the site. Store all decorations, signs, and materials which may be of use for future activities. Return all borrowed items in good condition.

Have a gathering for all workers as soon as possible. Serve a meal or

refreshments. Everyone should be con-
gratulated on a job well done and thanked
as a group by the general chairperson. The
gathering will also provide an opportunity
for the workers to be thanked individually
by their committee chairpersons. Give a
report on the success of the project and
promise details after the committee reports
are gathered.

Every worker and every individual
and business that donated money, equip-
ment, merchandise, or time should receive a verbal and written thank you *as
soon as possible.* Not only is this practice good manners, it builds goodwill for
future fundraising projects. When writing success stories to send the media,
don't forget to identify those who sponsored the event or made significant
contributions to it.

Gather detailed written reports from all committees. These reports
should be considered as the event leaders evaluate every aspect of the project. This review process should include dividing the profit made by the estimated hours worked by everyone to determine the return-per-hour received
by the organization. This information needs to be considered when making
future plans. A summary report should be prepared for the general membership. This report can include recommendations on whether the event should
be repeated and what changes could or should be made. Presentation of a
check might accompany the report and recommendations.

Valuing Non-Monetary Benefits

Some organizations believe that special fundraising events have only
one purpose—to make a reasonable profit. Other fundraisers place a high
value on the non-monetary benefits received from their money making projects. Such possible benefits are numerous. The event can, for example, provide publicity for the organization and the cause, and promote goodwill among
members of the community. It provides a time for members of the community to interact and have fun together in a positive context, and it may bring
new people into the organization. Working together instills a sense of fel-
lowship and group identity in the volunteers, yet individuals simultaneously
get personal satisfaction from contributing to the worthy cause. And special
event projects develop leadership skills.

The value placed on non-monetary benefits will influence planning for
future fundraisers.

FUNDRAISING IDEAS

A-THONS

A-thons (actually a suffix appropriated from the word "marathon" for application to any endurance event) are events during which participants do an activity for a certain extended distance or time, or for as long as they can. Some of the more common types are walk-a-thons, run-a-thons and bike-a-thons.

Prior to the event, participants enlist as many sponsors as possible. Sponsors pledge to pay an amount of money based on how much the participant does—for example, a dime, quarter, or dollar for each mile walked. The participant collects the pledges after the event and turns in the money to the organization or charity.

Sometimes prizes are given to the participants. The prizes may be inexpensive items for all who raise a minimum amount of money or nicer awards for those who collect the most money. Prizes can be numerous things. Many times a business or individual will donate prizes or provide them at nominal cost. Examples of prizes include T-shirts, water bottles, trophies, certificates of achievement, raffle tickets, radios, stereos, etc.

An event which attracts a large crowd may allow you to sell admission tickets. Cold drinks and other food items can be sold. Sell raffle tickets before and during the event and give away the raffle items at a concluding awards ceremony. If you can, enlist celebrities or other well-known people in the community to be participants. They often obtain larger pledges and attract a crowd.

All participants in the event should receive written information which states the date, time, place, all rules and a description of prizes and the conditions for winning them. Provide instructions for enlisting sponsors, collecting the money after the event and turning in the money. Have a form to be used for recording the names, addresses and phone numbers of sponsors. The form should also have a column for the amount pledged, amount owed, and date collected.

Be creative in deciding on an event appropriate for your group. The following are activities your participants might do:

- bat-a-thon (hit balls from a pitching machine)
- bike-a-thon
- carry-a-thon (walk with a cup of water balanced on head)
- dance-a-thon
- diet-a-thon (pay for pounds lost)
- eat-a-thon (amount of some food eaten in time given—such as pizza)
- egg-a-thon (toss and catch a raw egg)
- fish-a-thon
- hop-a-thon (children hopping during 2 or 3 minutes)
- jump-a-thon (jumping a rope)
- play-a-thon (playing a musical instrument)
- read-a-thon
- rock-a-thon (rocking in a rocking chair)
- run-a-thon (or marathon)
- sing-a-thon
- skate-a-thon
- ski-a-thon
- swim-a-thon
- twirl-a-thon (twirl a baton)
- waddle-a-thon (walk with balloon between knees)
- walk-a-thon

Workers will need to be organized to deal with publicity, registration of participants, prizes, preparation and clean-up of the site, handling of money and any supporting activities for raising money (such as raffles, food sales, and photographs).

Success story: Hike for the Homeless

ACCESSORIES BOOTH

An accessories booth needs many items in a wide variety of colors. Unless you have a very inexpensive supply of quality wholesale items or a dealer who will take returns of what does not sell, concentrate on selling homemade accessories or enhancing inexpensive items by decorating them. Items to make or decorate include tote bags, shoe bags, lunch bags, head and neck scarves, hats, eyeglass cases, covered or plastic headbands, umbrellas, nylon wallets, hair ties, barrettes, mittens, shawls, collars, belts, button covers, corsages, and jewelry.

Related fundraising idea: Crafts Booth

AD SPACE

Publications and programs offer the opportunity to sell ad space. High school yearbooks, newspapers, and play programs can provide places for students to sell ads to businesses. Member directories for an organization are appropriate for ad space. Each time the organization produces a publication of any type, consider whether an ad sales campaign is a good fundraising idea.

Ads are usually priced by their size, so you need a price list for the sizes you are offering. It is a good idea to make up some sample ads for businesses and sponsors who want suggestions. Business cards may be enlarged or shrunk and used for an ad. Many businesses have ads already in use that they will place in a publication sponsored by a worthy cause.

ANIMAL WORLD BOOTH

Some entire stores are devoted to items featuring one animal, such as cows or teddy bears. Having items related to any animal offers more possibilities.

Stuffed animals are popular with toddlers and teenagers and some adults. T-shirts, sweatshirts, tote bags, signs, umbrellas—all sorts of merchandise—can be decorated with pictures or words about animals. Photograph posters of animals with clever captions, books about animals, and ceramic animals are just a few of the possibilities.

Related fundraising idea: Pet Booth
Resource: Dover Publications, Inc.

ANTIQUE SHOW

An antique show may do well if your community is an area where many people appreciate items which are over a hundred years old or reproductions of antiques.

Sell space in an auditorium, gym, or hall to dealers and collectors so they can display their wares.

Charge admission so even the people who only come to look contribute to your income.

You can, or course, sell food items, have a crafts booth, offer items for a raffle, etc.

To attract a larger crowd, you might advertise door prizes requiring the person to be present to win and select prizes attractive to those who appreciate antiques.

ART SHOW

A chairperson who is very knowledgeable about art and acquainted with art shows is necessary for this project.

A second requirement is appropriate arrangements for displaying the art that is for sale. The group can charge the artist for a display area and or offer to sell the art of those artists who cannot or do not wish to sell their own art.

If you sell art for an artist, select your art carefully and charge a commission. Artists need to sign a release giving the organization permission to show and sell their work on consignment.

Provide enough workers to insure no harm comes to the art. Provide a program indicating the artists and the types of work shown. Try to have one or more artists present working on a piece of art. An entrance fee which includes simple refreshments can be charged.

ARTIST BOOTH

An artist who produces line drawings, charcoal drawings, or silhouette cuttings of customers can raise funds with very little overhead expense. An artist might also display his or her works for sale and give the fundraisers a percentage of any sales. First find a willing artist and then work out a mutually satisfactory agreement.

AUCTION

Auctions can take many forms depending on what will work for the sponsoring group. They are not just sales but also entertainment for observers. The merchandise can be of one special type or a variety of items. The goal is to have the auctioned items donated by individuals or businesses. A professional auctioneer who will donate the time is ideal, but a local celebrity or well-known person or "funny" organization member can do very well. If you have amateurs filling the auctioneer's spot, let them take turns and perhaps compete with each other to see who can raise the most money or obtain the highest price of the evening.

Auctions are fundraisers that can be managed by a small, dedicated group of workers, if needed. It is important that they begin soliciting items to auction as early as possible and in a planned, organized manner. Anything can be auctioned: antiques; white elephants (like-new items, unused by the owner); needlework, such as quilts, afghans, or hooked rugs; framed original paintings or photographs; certificates for free meals; passes to a swimming pool, bowling alley, amusement park, etc.; tickets for ballgames, plays, rodeos, etc.; subscriptions to the local paper; gourmet foods; catered dinners; use of a condo in a resort area; autographed books or photographs of a celebrity.

Although some items will bring a high price because of spirited competition or the skills of the auctioneer, many bidders are looking for bargains and often the contribution to the fundraising is shared by the person donating an item and the purchaser.

Success stories: Auction; Flea Market and Auction; Strawberry Festival

AUCTION—SILENT

A silent auction can be fast and fun. Divide your collected items into several tables or "groupings"; use large numbers or letters which can be used by all to identify the table. Each item for sale needs a number and a corresponding bid sheet and pencil. Indicate on each bid sheet the minimum bid which will be accepted. At the beginning of the silent auction, allow a period for viewing the items and making bids. Have a person, preferably with a microphone, begin with table 1 (or A) and announce that the bidding for items on table 1 will end in 10 minutes. At the end of the 10 minutes, the person in charge announces that the table is closed, that the individual who has the high bid on each card should take the card and the item to the check-out table to pay the amount he or she bid. Workers at the checkout table should give the high bidder a receipt for the item. This process is followed for each consecutive table or grouping.

Try to have popular items distributed among the table groups to keep the interest high. Have tactful but responsible workers monitoring each table; assertive bidders can create some interesting situations.

The sale of food and a place for visiting is attractive for non-bidders and for those who have finished bidding and are waiting to see if they are the high bidders.

Related fundraising idea: Auction
Success story: Auction

BABYSITTING SERVICE

Secure volunteers willing to babysit and donate their income to the worthy cause. In addition to short term babysitting, try to offer child care for weekends and longer periods (utilizing a team of volunteers) in the child's home. This is a good fundraiser for grandparent-age volunteers to do in couples or pairs. Make clear that it is the parents' responsibility to interview, check references, and approve the workers provided.

BAKE SALE

A bake sale can be a fundraiser on its own or one performed in conjunction with almost any other event. If group members donate the baked goods, overhead is very little. The materials for the baked goods can also be purchased, with the volunteers donating the work of creating the final product. A kitchen at the site of the sale lends itself to baking on the spot so that the aroma will entice customers.

Pay careful attention to the packaging so that it will be as attractive as possible. Keep prices in the "bargain" range.

Check with large stores, shopping areas, banks, schools and churches to try to get permission to have a bake sale on their property during a high traffic time. In shopping areas, Saturdays are traditional bake sale days.

Success story: Bazaar

BAKE SALE BOOTH

A bake sale booth should cater to shoppers looking for instant nourishment and to those buying items to take home. If you can offer tables, or at least seats, you might sell pie and or cake by the slice and coffee and punch to drink. Have a good supply of paper plates, napkins and plastic forks and calculate their cost in your price. Don't forget to have a mop and other clean-up items handy. If customers must eat as they stand or walk, specialize in brownies, cookies, and other easy-to-handle baked items.

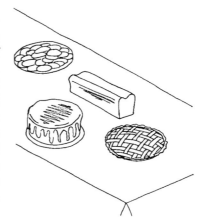

Good "take home" baked goods are breads, cakes, cupcakes, cookie assortments, pies, coffee cakes, muffins, cheesecake, jelly rolls, etc. Secure containers ahead of time and supply them to the cooks. Look for an economical supply that will be attractive and protect the baked item. Consider decorating the containers to make them more attractive and appropriate for gifts.

If possible, arrange to have the bake sale booth available to those who arrive at the event early. They can eat and drink coffee and juice while they wait for opening time. Keep records for how the various items sell so you will have a guide for quantities needed for the next bake sale booth.

BALLOONS—ANIMALS

Long thin balloons can be twisted into animals as children watch. If you want to make money, consider the time needed for each creation when you set your price. You may want to offer this attraction more as a way to entertain the children and have a nominal price.

Costumes for the workers add to the fun. Have someone talented train a number of people, since this tends to be tiring and breaks are needed. Production can be increased if helpers provide the blown-up balloons to the person creating the animals.

Related fundraising ideas: Carnival; Circus Theme
Resources: Piccadilly Books; St. Louis Carnival Supply

BALLOON BOUQUETS

Offer helium balloon bouquets as an alternative to flowers. Make a number of sample "arrangements," take a picture of each, set your price, enlist the workers who will make and deliver the bouquets, advertise, take orders and deliver.

This can be a specialized operation or an ongoing one. The group might only offer the balloon bouquets for hospital delivery or limit the project to Mother's Day, Father's Day, Secretary's Day, Valentine's Day, or some other special occasion.

Resources: St. Louis Carnival Supply; STUMPS—One Party Place

BALLOONS—HELIUM

Any event where children are present is an opportunity to sell helium balloons.

The balloons can have printed designs, be decorated by an artistic worker, have added faces, or have names added to order. If you want to add names, be sure to practice with the markers you will use. Brightly colored ribbon or yarn strings, in coordinating colors, will add to the appearance of the balloons.

While the salespersons can travel around, a central location where the balloons are inflated as they are needed is necessary. If you have a choice of places to obtain your balloons and helium, be sure to compare cost and rental terms. Ask if your worthy cause is eligible for a discount. Clown costumes, cheerleading uniforms, funny hats or other attention-getting clothing will help the balloon sales group stand out from the crowd and have fun. Send them out in pairs with one prepared to handle the money and give change. You can of course sell from a booth.

Resources: St. Louis Carnival Supply; STUMPS—One Party Place

BASKETS BOOTH

Baskets are a very versatile product. They can be decorated and lined or filled with flower arrangements, fruits, baked goods, Easter eggs, and all sorts of things.

Frequently, people will donate baskets they are not using to a fundraising effort. Often you can also buy baskets cheaply at garage and yard sales.

However, to have enough baskets to sustain a booth you must locate an inexpensive supply of baskets to be decorated and filled.

Baskets decorated and filled to reflect holiday themes are often in demand. Besides the obvious Christmas and Easter themes, consider all holidays, such as Halloween, Thanksgiving, St. Patrick's Day, Fourth of July, etc.

Related fundraising ideas: Food Booth; Country Style Booth

Resource: Sterling Publishing Company, Inc.

BATTLE OF THE SEXES

Establish two large clear containers in a convenient location and mark one "Men" and one "Women." Announce a battle to see which group can win under the following rules: Men are to put pennies in their container and women are to put pennies in their container; each penny counts toward their total money and the group with the most money will be declared the winner. However, any silver coins—nickels, dimes, quarters, half-dollars—deposited in a container by the opposing group are deducted from the value of the pennies in determining the winner.

BAZAARS

Bazaar, carnival, fair and festival are all terms used broadly by fundraising groups to represent an event which features a variety of entertainments and items for sale to benefit a worthy cause.

This section concentrates on events which emphasize the sale of all manner of merchandise. If you are considering having games, side shows, and rides as part of your bazaar, read the section on **Carnivals** for suggestions. Ideas for organizing exhibitions and displays are presented under the heading of **Fairs**. Performance possibilities are discussed in the **Festivals** section.

Bazaars are very hard work and require many volunteers. Do not even begin unless you have a core of dependable, dedicated workers and the potential of others to help them. The positive side of the hard work and involvement of numerous individuals is that a bazaar is an excellent means of uniting the group as they work for a common cause.

Planning must be completed and implemented under the direction of a capable leader. The leader should gather key workers and make the following decisions about the bazaar as a group: date, place, hours, number and types of booths and supporting activities, a theme (if desired), budget with estimated costs, source of funds for expenses, anticipated revenue from plans, committees needed, a publicity plan, whether or not to charge admission, and other decisions relative to the group's unique situation. From the beginning of planning, a qualified and trusted person must be in charge of all money matters and the keeping of financial records.

Fall is the prime time for a bazaar. It avoids the hottest weather, most people are home from vacation, and many are thinking about Christmas shopping. Spring is the next best choice with the merchandise leaning toward warm weather activities and events. Most bazaars are on weekends when both workers and customers are most likely to not be at their places of employment or at school.

A bazaar needs a large space—indoors, outdoors, or both. Just remember that the weather occurs on nature's schedule and you must have a backup indoor plan of anything scheduled to be outside. In choosing your location, consider where your customers will park. A shuttle service may be appropriate.

Draw a simple but accurate diagram which provides for all booths and stations and analyze the locations in relation to desired traffic flow. Prominent signs should point the way to the various sections and most frequently used locations. An information booth is needed near the main entrance or in a central location.

Committees that function effectively are one of the keys to a successful bazaar. Part of enlisting committee chairpersons can be surveying all members of the organization to see how they prefer to help and whom they can enlist to work with them. Most people will help with the group's project if they can do something they enjoy or work with other people they like. After establishing committees for each booth and major task, the director of the bazaar needs to communicate regularly with the various chairperson and keep abreast of plans, progress, and problems in all areas. This avoids duplication of effort and develops the feeling of all workers being a team.

Responsibilities of chairpersons will vary greatly. For example, the person in charge of handicrafts will be working for months to see that appropriate items are available for sale. The chairperson of the bake sale will be lining up people to donate or bake items for sale but cannot prepare the actual product until shortly before the bazaar begins. What all chairpersons will have in common is the need to plan carefully, enlist adequate helpers for all stages of the work, maintain accurate records and keep the director informed.

Customers may buy something purely to support the worthy cause, but in order to have enthusiastic buyers you need a wide variety of quality items. Unusual items, handmade products, and things perceived as bargains are usually best sellers. Preparing merchandise to sell at a bazaar is a challenge, and your variety is limited only by the imagination and energy of those doing the work.

Even workers who are not especially skilled at making items to sell can contribute by working sessions under the supervision of an organized leader who is talented at both making and teaching. Gather the materials, instructions, and samples and make creating handcrafted items a fun social occasion. These working times should take place as long before the bazaar as possible. If you have a yearly event, hold these sessions often and year-round with many kinds of projects and several leader-teachers.

Ideas for items to sell may be found in how-to books in libraries and bookstores, women's magazines, pattern books, and craft store racks. In addition to new items, certain throwaway or inexpensive items can be transferred into attractive, salable items with simple additions if the work is done well.

Give away or sell shopping bags for a nominal amount. They can be at every booth or provided by roving sellers. If possible, have the organization's name and a symbol of the bazaar theme on the bags. Look for a supplier to furnish bags or buy them wholesale. If you can't arrange printing at a reasonable cost, consider having volunteers decorate the bags with felt tip markers or tape on a colorful duplicated label with the information you want on the bags. This is good advertising and an appreciated service for those spending their money at your event. The shopping bag might be tied to a nominal admittance fee.

Demonstrations often are part of selling articles. Items made or finished while customers watch often stimulate sales. Think about the steps required to create an item and consider whether one or several can be demonstrated at the booth. Personalizing of items often works well using some of the same supplies needed to demonstrate.

Periodic door prizes and raffles add interest to the schedule.

It is often a good idea to use tickets or tokens in place of money for many booths. A good price for the tickets is one which will lend itself to convenience—perhaps $.10, $.25, and $1. Have the vendors price their goods accordingly. Consider opening the night before the bazaar or two hours early and charging an admission fee for early buying privileges.

Provide as many services as you can that will be appreciated by your customers. Don't forget to provide chairs or benches for "rest centers." In cold weather, provide free and convenient cloakrooms. The parking lot may need people to direct traffic. Can you furnish a supervised playground or nursery for young children? Provide access to food and a place to sit for those who arrive before opening time.

At the end of your bazaar, don't give away or return any leftover merchandise. Try to find some way to sell it for some amount or pack it for the next bazaar or fundraising event. Also keep decorations and props which are in good condition or repairable for future use.

For overall bazaar theme ideas see the following topics in this section: **Christmas Theme; Circus Theme; Country Theme; Early American Theme; Fourth of July Theme; Good Ole Days Theme; Hawaiian Theme; International Theme; South of the Border Theme; Spring Theme.**

Related fundraising ideas: Accessories Booth; Animal World Booth; Artists Booth; Bake Sales Booth; Balloons—Animals; Balloons—Helium; Baskets Booth; Books Booth; Boutique Booth; Cake Sale; Calendars; Candy—Homemade; Caramel Apples and Popcorn Balls; Children's Art Make and Take; Children's Corner Booth; Children's Dress-Up Booth; Children's Hats and Makeup Booth; Christmas Booth; Christmas Cookie Trays; Cookbooks; Country Style Booth; Crafts Booth; Flea Market Booth; Food Booth; Hamburger Stand; Hatters; Herbs & Spices Booth; Hobbies Booth; Hot Dog Stand; Jewelry Booth; Kitchen Booth; Makeup Booth; Moving Booths; Needlework Shop; Personalized Items Booth; Pet Booth; Photographs Booth; Photographer—Moving; Plant and Flower Booth; Popcorn; Portrait Center; Red, White and Blue Booth; Sand Art Booth; Sayings and Quotes Booth; Shirts Booth; Toys Booth; Victorian Booth; Wood Products Booth; Yard Booth.
Success Stories: Arts and Crafts Fair; Bazaar; Christmas Craft Fair.

BEAUTY CONTEST—MEN ONLY

Enlist as many men as possible to appear in drag for a beauty contest. Have an entry fee, perhaps paid by business or individual sponsors. Plan the contest so it will provide unique entertainment and then advertise and sell tickets. A printed program will provide an opportunity to sell ad space.

A bathing suit modeling is a must. For a talent section, have someone prepared with suggestions for the entrants who need help. Suggestions could be a poetry reading, reciting a nursery rhyme dramatically, displaying an artistic creation, etc. The talent segment might be replaced by a joke telling contest if you can trust the contestants to use good taste and still be funny. Some mock "heavy questions" can be prepared for all or finalists.

To determine the winners, enlist a panel of prominent people to rate each contestant and have someone total the scores of all the judges. Another approach is to have the audience vote on a ballot which comes with their purchase of admission. For a very popular cause, the members of the audience might even buy votes for their favorite entrant. The selling of votes could be done during an intermission during which food is also available for sale.

A talented master or mistress of ceremonies and live music would add to the show. A show director and a practice are necessary so the show will keep moving and maintain the interest of the audience.

The winner needs a crown, a medallion on a ribbon around his neck or a ribbon banner across his chest, a "walk" to be presented to the crowd and an official picture.

Beauty contests are, of course, ideas for traditional events for women and girls of all ages. The title bestowed can be "Queen of —" (name of the town, festival, parade, etc.).

Related fundraising idea: Ad Space
Success story: Men's Beauty Contest

BINGO

Bingo is a form of gambling and illegal in some areas. Where it is legal, it is controlled by local and state laws. Before planning a fundraiser which includes bingo, carefully research and understand all laws and regulations.

Bingo to raise money can range from a one night event with a variety of donated prizes to a regular weekly project which attracts the serious bingo player as well as those who participate for occasional recreation. Serious bingo games seem to offer cash prizes and utilize sophisticated equipment to operate the games. Organized volunteers are needed for each bingo session and regular volunteers need to accept the responsibility of supervision and troubleshooting.

A bingo event can be operated with inexpensive bingo sets and a caller who keeps track on a master card. Each game can be played for a specific prize or the winner can choose from a selection of prices. If you have several exceptionally nice prizes, reserve them for the end of the evening and allow each person who wins a session to have his or her name placed in a container. A drawing will then determine who receives the grand prizes.

Success story: Bingo
Resource: Midwest Bingo

BOOK FAIR

Secondhand books are relatively easy to acquire by donation and inexpensive purchases at garage sales and flea markets. An energetic organization can conduct a yearly book fair and realize a good profit. The group needs adequate room and a convenient location for displaying tables and shelves of books they have collected. Book wholesalers and retailers may be willing to provide new books on consignment. Divide the books by types—paperback and hardcover, old and new, romance, mysteries, science fiction, how-to, self-help, etc. Make the prices low and offer a discount for purchases of three or more books. Save the leftovers for the next fair if you have storage space; books which do not sell in two fairs should probably be discarded. Keep records which will indicate to the committee what types of books sell best for your event and put extra energy into collecting those categories of books. If you identify a good source of book donations, have a volunteer make a personal contact to express appreciation and to ask for donations for the next book fair.

Related fundraising idea: Books Booth
Success story: Book Fair

BOOKS BOOTH

Collect books of all kinds constantly and buy cheaply those with potential at garage and yard sales and flea markets. This will give you a good start on the merchandise for a books booth. Keep your prices low. One good method is to have two or three prices and group the books that are the same price together. Consider giving a discount for multiple buys, such as: $.25 each or five for $1, or buy two and get one free.

Sell new books if the supplier will allow you to return those not sold.

You might have a table for old magazines that have been donated. In addition to books offer items such as bookmarks, bookracks, bookends, book and Bible covers, photo albums, scrapbooks, calendars and other items you would expect to see for sale in a bookstore.

Related fundraising idea: Book Fair
Resource: Dover Publications, Inc.

BOUTIQUE BOOTH

Attractively display used clothes. Make sure all your clothes are clean and mend them where it is practical. Hang as many of the clothes as you can on hangers and fold the others neatly on the tables. Sort by men's, women's, boys' and girls' wear. Price everything low because everyone will be looking for a bargain. Have as much room as possible. Provide full-length mirrors and a fitting room if you can. Include accessories such as purses, hats, scarves, wallets, jewelry and shoes in good shape, if you have them. After the sale, consider keeping only the most salable items for next time and donating the rest to a charity which distributes clothes to the poor all year round.

Related fundraising ideas: Flea Market Booth; Rummage Sales; Thrift Shop

BREAKFAST IN BED—DELIVERED

Advertise a service of delivered breakfast-in-bed for Mother's Day. All order forms should specify one of the offered menu choices and a time range for delivery—as well as the name, address, and telephone number of both the recipient and the person placing the order. This will probably work best if the order is paid for and a receipt given with a money back guarantee. Provide a Mother's Day card to be completed by the person placing the order and delivered with the breakfast. Have a person who is very detail oriented  plan the preparation and delivery schedule and have several people review the schedule for possible problems. Be sure the delivery people have good maps and directions and all the materials they need to care for the condition of the food.

Plan carefully how the breakfast can be delivered in good condition. Hot items and cold items must be kept separate until they reach their destination, and efforts must be made to keep them at the desired temperature. The cold items will need to be transported in a cooler. Include microwave instructions with hot items in case they need warming. The tray, dishes, and utensils should be as elegant as possible while still being disposable. A small vase of real flowers for the tray would be nice.

Related fundraising ideas: Dinner Delivered; Lunch Delivered/Packed

CAKE SALE

Cake sales can be held almost anywhere. They can be in a booth, after a meeting, at a shopping area, at a sporting event—anywhere there is a crowd and a place to display the cakes.

Sell whole cakes and or cake by the slice. If possible have tables for those eating on the spot and offer ice cream as a topping. Serve coffee, hot tea, hot chocolate, and milk to drink with the cake.

Offer the recipe for specialty cakes and directions for cakes that are cut and decorated to look like animals. If you want to add related products, consider cookbooks, recipe cards, recipe holders, decorating tools, books on cake decorating, and special shaped cake pans.

CAKEWALKS

Cakewalks are an old tradition for school carnivals and can be used at many events. Cakes are donated. Numbers are placed on the floor in a circle—large numbers written on masking tape with a black marker work well. Participants pay money to take part in the walk and each stands on a number. The "walk" consists of the participants walking around the circle, on the numbers, to music (use a portable tape player) and stopping on a number when the music stops after a brief period. The person in charge of the cakewalk then has one of the numbers drawn from a container; the person standing on the number wins the cake offered.

After the cake is given to the winner each time, the process is repeated as frequently as the number of cakes and customers allows.

CALENDARS

Seek a wholesale source for calendars for members to sell in the fall of the year. Consider whether one style or a variety will be a better product for your group. Offering calendars in attractive boxes or gift-wrapped should promote their purchase for gift purposes.

CANDY—HOMEMADE

The existence of various businesses thriving on candy sales alone testifies to the appeal of candy as a product. Homemade candy, particularly any version of fudge, offers the potential of good profits for the group with cooks willing to produce the candy for a fundraising event. If possible, have some of the ingredients donated, perhaps by those who do not help make the candy. Containers are important for sales. Collect pretty but inexpensive dishes, mugs, and boxes for packaging some of the candy. The candy not sold in a container can be wrapped well and have a ribbon or other decoration attached.

CAR WASH

Cleaning cars is traditionally a teenage fundraising activity, probably because it is so active. However, adults should be present, involved and responsible.

The location for a car wash should have a fairly large hard-surfaced area that can tolerate being soaked with water for a long period of time. One or more hoses attached to a good supply of water are mandatory. Supplies needed include buckets, gentle soap which will not damage paint, soft brushes, and many rags. Vacuums and dry brushes, as well as buckets of water and rags, are needed for cleaning car interiors.

Furnish waiting customers a place to sit. You may want to provide or sell coffee and sodas. Newspapers and magazines to read might be appreciated. One or two people should handle the money. If you have enough help, someone might keep a record of the types of vehicles and the times they arrive and the times they leave. The time log would ensure that someone notes slow service and also provide information for planning any future car wash events.

This fundraising project is low on investment but demands good publicity, an accessible location, and the availability of high energy labor.

Success story: Car Wash

CARAMEL APPLES & POPCORN BALLS

In early October prepare samples and take orders for caramel apples and or caramel popcorn balls to be delivered for Halloween events. If you have individuals experienced in preparing these items, put them in charge of work sessions to prepare and package the apples and popcorn balls ordered. If no workers have experience with caramel apples and caramel popcorn balls, they can learn by using several recipes from cookbooks as they prepare samples. Other workers can organize to deliver the orders.

These items can also be the feature item at a stationary or roving booth at any event.

CARD MAILING SERVICE

Forgetful or very busy people might sign up for a greeting card mailing service. This service takes a significant amount of time for the volunteers and

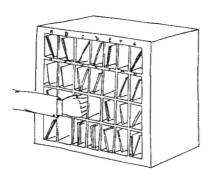

customers to establish, but very little time to renew in future years. The customer completes a form indicating the name, address, kind of card (occasion and style—sincere, funny, conservative), and date to be mailed for each card needed. The workers gather the greeting cards requested for the year and meet with the customer for approval and signatures. A volunteer who has an attractive handwriting addresses and stamps the cards which are then carefully filed under the dates they are to be mailed. One of the most important parts of this service is to be *sure* the cards are faithfully mailed as promised.

An alternative to the workers selecting the cards is to enlist a card shop to make available cards for all seasons for a two week period when the customer selects and purchases his or her cards for the service to mail. Either the customer or the fundraisers could expect a discount from the business supplying the cards.

The most profitable time for this service will be Christmas. Businesses and professional people might hire a service they expected to operate for at least several years.

CARD PARTIES

Plan a big event around the community's favorite card game or plan a series of card parties. Have a card party in the afternoon aiming for customers who are homemakers or retired or have it on a Friday or Saturday night when it can be an "evening out." Play bridge, gin rummy, pinochle, canasta, Skip-Bo, or any other card game. Why not offer a separate room where group members give lessons?

Be sure your rules are clear, offer prizes, and provide hosts to be sure everything goes smoothly and keep the customers happy. You might have a theme and an entertainment and refreshment break during the party. A raffle would be compatible with a card party. Just take care that the admission covers all expenses and provides an acceptable profit.

CARNIVAL

Carnival, bazaar, fair and festival are all terms used broadly by fundraising groups to represent an event which features a variety of entertainments and items for sale to benefit a worthy cause. This section presents ideas for a collection of entertainments, such as games, side shows, rides and refreshments. If you are interested in information about the sale of all manner of merchandise, see **Bazaars**. Ideas for organizing exhibitions and displays are presented under **Fairs**. Performance possibilities are discussed in relation to **Festivals**.

Games of skill which offer a prize are often the heart of a carnival. It is best to have a ticket booth which sells tickets which are used for playing the games. If the carnival is for all ages, have a special section reserved for the very young and a few games designed to challenge adults. Several people should try out all the games of skill after they are set up to help set the price and rules. The players should have a fair opportunity to win a prize but not be able to make the game unprofitable for the group.

Prizes can be simple and compatible with the price to play and the difficulty of winning. Try for donated prizes and supplement with carefully chosen inexpensive prizes and those bought at wholesale or bargain prices. Inexpensive prizes might include balloons, balls, wrapped candy, fancy erasers, gum, headbands, magnets, pencils, pens, flashlights, jewelry, etc. Shop at carnival supply stores and at dollar stores for items. Instead of many small items, you might have a prizes "store." Each booth could give tokens to winners and they could trade in tokens toward prizes at the store. In this case, the prizes would range from nominal to more valuable, such as radios, stuffed animals, games, etc.

Games of skill are easy to create. They may be purchased or made. The following are a few classic examples: dropping clothespins into a jar; tossing bean bags into containers; ring toss; picking up jelly beans with chopsticks; hammering nails into a 2 × 4; digging in a pan of sand for a small toy (for small children); indoor basketball shooting; knocking down plastic bottles with a ball; blowing out candles with a water pistol. Check your library game books for ideas.

Side shows could include acrobatic routines, clown acts, dance exhibitions, fashion shows (serious and for fun), fortune telling, jugglers, magic shows, musicians (singing and instrumental), puppets, and storytellers. Side show acts should give free "teasers" of their show between performances. This should attract larger crowds and add interest to the carnival site.

Carnivals frequently have activities which fall into no specific category. A weight guessing booth, for example, can be fun with the right operator. The prizes can be worth less than the cost to play, thus ensuring a profit. Face or body painting is popular and can be done by artists with modest skill if they limit their design offerings and practice. Offer chances to guess the number of beans or other small items in a jar. The person whose guess is closest wins a prize near the end of the carnival. This makes a good moving event. Many foods can be sold at a carnival. Traditional foods include hotdogs, popcorn, lemonade, and sodas. Pony rides are a sure hit with young children. And how about a super-safe ride on a tractor?

Related fundraising ideas: Balloons—Animals; Balloons—Helium; Cakewalks; Caramel Apples and Popcorn Balls; Children's Dress-Up Booth; Children's Hats and Makeup Booth; Fortunes; Hamburger Stand; Hot Dog Stand; Kissing Booth; Petting Place; Photographer Props; Pictures with Impersonators; Pony Rides; Strolling Musicians; Wet Sponge Throw.

Resources: Ace-Acme; Plays, Inc., Publishers; STUMPS—One Party Place; St. Louis Carnival Supply

CATERING CHILDREN'S PARTIES

Charge a basic fee, plus a set amount for each guest, to cater children's parties. A team of members would handle the entire preparations and direct the party. Include decorations, games, prizes, refreshments, and favors. Offer a set of photographs or a video recording of the event if you have someone who can provide this service. Provide customers an agreement sheet which outlines several party themes and the options which are available for each. Be sure an agreement specifying details of your service is signed for each party to prevent misunderstandings.

Most important of all, the members in charge of leading the party activities must be experienced with children and enjoy being with them.

Resources: Contemporary Drama Service; Eldridge Publishing Company; Lonestar Technologies, Ltd.; McFarland & Company, Inc., Publishers; Meriwether Publishing Ltd., Publisher; Play, Inc., Publishers; Piccadilly Books; The H.W. Wilson Company

CHARM SCHOOLS

Develop a charm course teaching subjects such as makeup to fit the occasion, hairstyles and hair care, healthy eating, selecting an exercise program, color analysis and wardrobe selection, personal clothing style, posture and graceful movement, voice quality and speaking style, conversation skills, time management, stress control, entertaining with ease, improving use of leisure time, etc.

Charm school could be the feature of a weekend retreat or could be taught Saturday mornings or one evening a week. Advertise the schedule and charge for the entire package of lessons in self-improvement. Use qualified members of the organization as instructors or utilize professionals who will donate their time or will work at a reasonable rate.

Related fundraising ideas: Color Analysis; Classes

CHILDREN'S ART—MAKE AND TAKE

Set up an area where children can make two or three kinds of pictures with the help of their parents or the older teens or adults running the booth.

Provide the tables, chairs and supplies needed and old shirts or aprons for the children to wear to protect their clothes. Be sure everything in the booth can be cleaned since a mess or two is to be expected. Have cleaning materials on hand. Charge by the picture; ask that parents stay close by and provide them with seats.

This type of booth can also be used to allow children to make a craft project, such as bookmarks, decorated paperweights, their names on precut paper hats, etc.

Resources: McFarland & Company, Inc., Publishers; Meredith Press Corporation; Pack-o-Fun; Sterling Publishing Co., Inc.

CHILDREN'S CORNER BOOTH

A Children's Corner booth can carry a large assortment of items. The main categories that come to mind are items for babies, children's clothing and toys. Baby items could include bibs, blankets, shawls, hats, mittens, gowns, booties, and similar items. Children's clothing would include decorated shirts, hair decorations, neckties, Halloween and other costumes, dress-up items like long skirts or capes—whatever children would like to wear or their parents or grandparents would like for them to wear.

Toys could range from busy-baby quilts, wooden animal toys, puzzles, and stuffed animals to dolls, doll clothes, bean bag games, and song tapes. Secondhand toys and games should be available from donors for the asking. Personalized items are usually good sellers. Include many inexpensive items which will appeal to children: balls, plastic people and animals, gum and candy, etc.

Resources: Chilton Book Company; Dover Publications, Inc.; Rodale Press, Inc.; Sterling Publishing Co., Inc.; Sunset Publishing Corporation

CHILDREN'S DRESS-UP BOOTH

Collect hats, scarves, high heels, boots, necklaces, capes, costume pieces and other items young children like to wear for playing. For a fee allow children to play in the booth under the supervision of adults who will help them with items they select to put on. Full length mirrors are needed so they can admire themselves.

Offer Polaroid pictures for a reasonable fee. Help any parents with their own camera to take pictures of their children in their fancy clothes.

Resource: Plays, Inc., Publishers

CHILDREN'S HATS AND MAKEUP BOOTH

Select several ways you can make up children to coordinate with a hat and create a special look. Make colored drawings of choices the children have or make up children ahead of time and display their pictures to show what is available.

Clowns, Gypsies, and Indians are appropriate for both boys and girls. Pirate, soldier, princess, and bride are other examples. Halloween costumes may provide ideas. Keeping the hat to wear is part of the charge. The hats can be made or bought in bulk. Experiment with makeup application ahead of time. Consider using theatrical makeup.

Polaroid pictures for those who want them would be an additional element to the fundraising effort.

Resources: Baker's Plays; St. Louis Carnival Supply; STUMPS—One Party Place

CHILDREN'S SHOPPING EVENT

A few weeks before Christmas, Mother's Day or Father's Day, provide a shopping opportunity for children to buy gifts for family and friends or mother or father. Provide a wide supply of inexpensive, colorful gifts. Allow no one over 12 to shop. Salespersons with patience and tact should be available to help and advise.

Items for sale can be donated by businesses and supporters or made by organization volunteers. Attractively packaged candy is a good item as are most craft items which can be sold for a modest amount of money. Provide something for every age person at Christmas and items appropriate for a mother or father just before their special day.

Advertise heavily and well in advance so parents can plan on their children shopping at your event and children can save money so they will be prepared to take advantage of your shopping service.

Related fundraising ideas: Crafts Booth; Christmas Booth

CHILDREN'S WEEKEND CAMP

Provide a weekend for paying children to eat, sleep, and participate in educational and fun activities. Seek volunteer camp workers and the donation of a place to have the camp. Someone experienced with supervising children needs to review the liabilities associated with caring for children and be sure to obtain parent permission forms and emergency information.

Resources: Contemporary Drama Service; Eldridge Publishing Company; Lonestar Technologies, Inc.; McFarland & Company, Inc., Publishers; Plays, Inc., Publishers; Sterling Publishing Co., Inc.; The H.W. Wilson Company

CHILI COOK-OFF DINNER

Enlist cooks who pride themselves on their ability to prepare wonderful chili to participate in a chili cook-off. The cost of entry is to donate the chili to a chili supper held at the end of the contest. The prizes can range from ribbons to something more substantial like a new chef's apron or coupons good for several dinners out for two. Enlist judges who declare winners after tasting all of the entries, which are identified only by number.

After the awarding of prizes, other volunteers take over and provide a meal featuring the chili. Crackers, relish dishes, desserts, etc. (perhaps donated) complement the chili. Customers pay for the meal. Entertainment could be provided.

CHRISTMAS BOOTH

No booth offers the potential for more items than a booth with a Christmas theme. If you need ideas, browse through stores, catalogs, craft stores, magazines, and even your collection of Christmas items. Keep your quality high, display the items attractively, and keep your prices at the bargain level.

Types of items to sell include ornaments of all kinds (try to display on

a tree); Christmas stockings of all shapes and sizes
(don't forget the family pet); tree skirts—ranging
from simple to elaborate; items such as tags, can
pencil holders, and collage pictures made from
old Christmas cards; pine cone Christmas trees,
centerpieces, and ornaments; wreaths of all
kinds; card holders; candles and holders; mantle
decorations; door decorations; hanging mistletoe
kissing balls; jewelry and corsages; table centerpieces; Santa and elf hats; Christmas cards and
stationery; wrapping paper and ribbon; gift
boxes and bags; Christmas tablecloths, placemats
and napkins; Christmas napkin-ring holders;
wooden items for the yard, such as a wooden snowman head on a stake or decorations with holes for lights or candy canes. Try a table of small items for stock-
ing stuffers for people of all ages. Food items like jelly, candy, and cookies packaged with Christmas colors in small quantities might do well here.

The possibilities are endless. If you include as many people as possible
in preparing the merchandise for this booth, you should have a good selection of items.

CHRISTMAS CAROLING

Have customers address and sign a Christmas card for your group to
deliver to those to be serenaded with Christmas carols.

Provide an agreement for your customer which specifies the date you
will carol, the songs (you might offer a choice), the number of songs, and the
charge (refundable in case of a blizzard). The agreement should state that you
cannot be responsible for the recipient of the caroling being home at the
specified time.

Since you are being paid, your caroling group should be made up of
singers who harmonize and sound good together. Practice sessions and a
planned standing arrangement are in order. Quality is more important than
the number of singers.

A large sign saying "Merry Christmas from —" and changeable sheets
indicating who sent you would be nice. After your selections, deliver the card
and give holiday greetings. Be sure all singers are dressed warmly so they will
not be miserable and distracted from their singing.

Resources; Lonestar Technologies, Ltd.; NTC Publishing Group

CHRISTMAS COOKIE TRAYS

Prepare an attractive tray of assorted homemade cookies as a sampler and use it, or a picture of it, to take orders. Have one price for a pickup on a certain day at a convenient time, but also try to offer a delivery service for a nominal fee. Include a gift card for those ordering the trays as gifts. Your order form should specify the number of cookies, price, and pickup or delivery details; it should also provide a place for the desired message if the tray is to be a gift.

Volunteers can bake cookies and donate them or a committee can buy the ingredients and have group baking sessions. Those who dislike baking can contribute by selling, packaging and delivering. Try for fresh baked cookies. If you freeze some for later delivery, be sure the ones you freeze taste fresh when thawed.

CHRISTMAS GIFT WRAPPING BOOTH

Seek permission and space in a shopping mall for a Christmas gift wrapping booth. Staff the booth with trained volunteers. An alternative is to advertise a drop-off and pickup service at specified times at a convenient location. Provide chairs, coffee, and magazines for those who prefer to wait. Seek donated or discount paper, tape, tags and bows. Some members might be willing to learn to make fancy bows to have on hand. Make prices reasonable but sufficient to cover costs and provide a profit.

Resources: Crown Publishers, Inc.; Leisure Arts

CHRISTMAS THEME

From middle November until December 25 it is hard to beat Christmas as a theme. The stores, media, and social events are geared toward the event and children of all ages are obsessed with the season. Decorations abound, often in the homes of group members. Buying of decorations, special foods, and gifts is rampant. Feelings of charity and goodwill are at their strongest. In many places the weather encourages indoor activities like fundraisers.

The most essential requirement for a group using a Christmas theme for an event to raise money is to start planning and making preparations many months in advance. The potential for this theme is so broad in every area that it is best to narrow the planning in the early stages and resist being distracted by other possibilities.

Related fundraising ideas: Christmas Booth; Christmas Caroling; Christmas Cookie Trays; Christmas Gift Wrapping Booth; Candy—Homemade; Card Mailing Service; Children's Shopping Event; Crafts Booth; Fruit Baskets; Portrait Center; Recorded Greetings; Toy Booth.

Success Story: Christmas Craft Fair

Resources: Eldridge Publishing Company; NTC Publishing Group

CIRCUS THEME

A large tent helps this theme, but it can be used outside or in a hall area. The costumes are fun for workers; there can be clowns of all descriptions, tightrope walkers, lion tamers, ring masters in top hats, etc. The circus theme is especially good when there are carnival type games of chance and side shows available. An animal show could be the main attraction. Perhaps a zoo or farm open to visitors could be persuaded to allow the group to use all or part of their facility.

Resources: Contemporary Drama Service; Meriwether Publishing Ltd.; Piccadilly Books

CLASSES

Money can be earned with classes of all kinds. The requirements are a good teacher, a topic or skill of interest being taught, students who will pay for the class, a place to meet, and the materials needed for the lesson(s). All of these requirements can be met by a resourceful and determined group. It is easiest if you start with either an available teacher or several people committed to a particular type of class. If you are short on ideas, take a survey, read advertisements in the Yellow Pages and newspapers, and obtain adult education and college schedules for inspiration.

While volunteer teachers who donate their services are great, don't rule out teachers who will work for a reasonable hourly fee or split the income in an acceptable way. Your contribution is to take care of everything except the actual teaching. Your project may be one lesson or a series. You may call your sessions workshops or seminars or demonstrations, as seems most appropriate.

The following list provides ideas for possible classes:

Acting
Auto Repair and Maintenance
Basic Home Repair
Business Skills (Basic Bookkeeping, Short-
  hand, Typing, Filing)
Cake Decorating
Calligraphy
Charm School
Cooking (Wok, Microwave, Crockpot,
  Ethnic)
Coping with Stress
CPR
Crafts (All kinds, such as quilting, crochet,
  ceramics, woodcrafts, silk screen art,
  papier-mâché, pottery dough art, stained
  glass items, print making, appliqué,
  English smocking, knitting)
Dancing (ballroom, tap, ballet, modern,
  belly dancing, square, line, country and
  western, etc.)
Dog Obedience
Drawing and Painting
English as a Second Language
Estate Planning and Records
Exercise/Aerobics
First Aid
Flower Arranging
Foreign Languages—Conversational Level
GED
Genealogy/Tracing Your Family Ancestors
Getting Published
Homemade Cosmetics
Jewelry Making
Job Hunting
Local History
Makeup Choices and Skills
Massage
Meditation Techniques
Music (reading music, voice, piano, guitar,
  etc.)
Photography
Purchasing a Home
Scarves as an Accessory
Self-Defense
Self-Defense for Women
Selling a Home
Shirt Decorating
Starting a Business
Taxes
Time Management
Tutoring Service
VCR Camera Projects
Weight Training
Yoga

Related fundraising ideas: Charm School; Color Analysis; Genealogy Workshops; Lectures

COLLEGE FINALS FOOD

Providing food to college students during final exams works best for groups who have access to the home addresses of students living in dorms or college housing and can do a mailing to parents. It could also work if several volunteers passed out advertising flyers at performances or sports events for a specific college or university. Another approach is an offer to mail parcel post packages to any student in any school and seek customers locally.

Busy students should like to receive items such as assorted fruit (fresh, dried or candied), small packages of snack mix, nuts, flavored popcorn, candy, homemade cookies, brownies, cocoa mix, gourmet coffee, and tea mixes. Warm pizza and cold soda, a cheesecake, a pie or a tin of homemade fudge are other ideas for products to deliver. Include several napkins, small paper plates and plastic utensils as appropriate. A card—perhaps a specially designed funny one—should be included telling who sent the package. Also include a phone number in case of problems with the package.

Inform the customer of the date you plan to deliver or mail the food and stick to your schedule.

COLOR ANALYSIS

Color analysis is the technique by which makeup consultants study a person's physical characteristics such as skin tone and eye and hair color to identify the colors of clothing and makeup that are most flattering for that individual. To base a fundraiser on this technique, collect cloth drapes in a variety of colors and hold color analysis sessions for a fee.

If you do not have someone available to you who is trained in color analysis, enlist three or four interested people to become competent in the color analysis process. This skill can be learned through reading and experience of analyzing individuals as a group. Your future experts might be able to attend a color analysis class or workshop.

The book *Color Me Beautiful* by Carole Jackson made the theory of color analysis and individual color seasons—spring, summer, autumn, winter—popular.

You might offer customers the opportunity to purchase or order books related to color analysis, color swatches for their season, basic items in the hard-to-find colors (basic blouses, scarves, suit handkerchiefs, etc., made by the group members or a professional seamstress). You will, of course, gear your sales to make money for your group.

Related fundraising idea: Charm School
Resources: Ballantine Books; Bantam Books, Inc.; Fashion Academy

CONCERTS

Frequently a band, choir, or vocalists will provide a benefit concert for a worthy cause. If you know of some group that could attract a crowd, ask if they are available. Your contribution is to provide a suitable site for the concert, do the advertising, sell the tickets, and see that the event runs smoothly.

Have a clear understanding with those providing the concert as to whether you owe them any expense money and whether they expect you to provide equipment or help in setting up. You may add additional fundraising events such as food sales or a raffle in conjunction with the concert.

COOKBOOKS

Many organizations have found it worthwhile to compile, print, and sell their own cookbook. The preparation of the material for a cookbook is very time consuming and should not be undertaken unless the group has many good cooks willing to work on the project. The recipes need to be unusual and interesting, and each of them should be tested to be sure they are reliable. After the recipes are collected and tested, someone will need to prepare the material for printing, organize the contents, write introductory copy, and arrange for artwork on the cover and as desired inside.

Check with local printers to gauge printing costs. Also consider using a company which specializes in publishing cookbooks for groups. Frequently you can obtain the name and address of a company from a cookbook being sold by some other organization on its own or in bookstores and write for information. Ad space in the cookbook can be sold to interested businesses and groups.

When the cookbook is ready, offer a copy to food editors for review and ask your local bookstores and other businesses to sell the book. Members can sell books individually and at all kinds of community meetings and events. A tasting party at which members offer samples of the various recipes could bring in funds through admission charges. Cookbooks would be offered for sale at the party.

After the cookbook is printed, its sales become a low-maintenance, long-term fundraising project.

Related fundraising idea: Ad Space
Resource: Cookbook Publishers, Inc.

COOKIE BOUQUETS

Decorated and shaped cookies attached to sticks of assorted lengths and wrapped in clear wrap can be assembled in a container like flowers to form a bouquet. Add ribbon and perhaps even silk greenery filler. Create and photograph several examples which your workers can create to order and offer them for sale for various occasions for which customers frequently purchase a flower bouquet. Accept orders based on your photographs. Have a bouquet suitable for someone ill, a birthday, Mother's Day, Father's Day, Secretary's Day, Valentine's Day, graduation, etc. Or you may want to have a seasonal sale with two or three choices appropriate for one specific holiday.

COUNTRY STYLE BOOTH

Country style is the basis for many gift shops and furniture stores. The merchandise can be what you make it.

If you have volunteers who like to work with wood items, enlist them to make items of all kinds. You can have shelves, plant holders, bookcases, stools, children's chairs, doll beds, bookends; virtually any wood product is appropriate for a country style booth.

Material, knit and crocheted items such as doll quilts, baby quilts, throws, shawls, afghans, doll clothes, dressed dolls and stuffed animals, sachets, pot holders, pillowcases, cushions, table cloths, placemats and similar items in country colors and prints can be sold.

Silk and dried flower arrangements in containers of all kinds in earthen colors can be offered. Potted ivy and house plants are appropriate. Wreaths can be made of many items as can wall decorations with the country look. If you have a "country store" corner you can offer stick candy, jelly, jam, apple butter, pickles, and other food items.

Resources: Chartwell Books; Chilton Book Company; Dover Publications, Inc.; Mallard Press; Smithmark Publishers, Inc.; Sterling Publishers Co., Inc.

COUNTRY THEME

One way for the planners of a fundraiser with a country theme to prepare for their task is to take time to walk through country style gift shops, flower shops, furniture stores, antique shops and similar places to develop a "feel" for the style.

At an event with a country theme there will be baskets, flower arrangements, items using calico material, quilts and needlework, and wooden items of all types. Decorations will be old or modern versions of old fashioned things like iron skillets, cornbread pans, churns, crock containers. Farm items like rakes and shovels, bales of hay, and dried corn can add to the country atmosphere. Jelly, preserves, molasses, stick candy, corn muffins, fried okra, fried chicken, and tea in fruit jars are the types of food brought to mind.

A country style theme is appropriate spring, summer or fall but seems most appropriate for fall, the harvest time of year.

Resources: Dover Publications, Inc.; STUMPS—One Party Place

COUPON BOOKS

If you are in an urban area, check the Yellow Pages for companies that have assembled coupon books which your organization can sell for a profit. The coupons in the books offered should be for free and discounted food, admissions, merchandise, and services which will attract a wide variety of customers. Be sure you can return books you do not sell.

You can create your own coupon books to sell, but be aware that this takes a significant number or hours to arrange the agreements with businesses and expenses for printing. An envelope of coupons good for a year might be a good alternative to having a book printed. The coupons could be provided by the business or created on a computer and copied and cut by the organization.

CRAFTS BOOTH

A crafts booth allows merchandise of all kinds. Volunteers donating their work can make their favorite items, use up scraps and still enjoy trying some-

thing new. Especially gifted craft creators can be used to supervise and teach the less creative in fun creating sessions. As a general rule, make products that look special or expensive but do not take a great deal of time. Look for everyday items which can be made elegant—such as covering the lids of baby food jars to create containers for spices or herbs.

If someone donates an item which required extensive labor and must be priced high, consider using it as a raffle item. Quilts, tablecloths, afghans and bedspreads are in this category. The following list of possible products is in no particular order and is designed only to spark ideas: cloth covered photo albums; decorated picture frames; stuffed animals; dolls; doll houses; doll furniture; clothes for dolls and stuffed animals; appliance covers; place mats; windsocks of all styles and sizes; stained glass suncatchers and tree ornaments; tissue box covers; tote and shoe bags; purses; eyeglass cases; throw pillows; decorated towels; bath wraps; covered hangers; banks; neckties; paperweights; mobiles; wrap and elastic waist skirts; decorated shirts; candles; centerpieces; sachets; covered matches; framed pictures, photographs, quilt blocks, sayings, or quotes; sculptures; paintings; pottery; handmade jewelry (such as from buttons); "touch me" books for babies; plain anklets decorated with lace, bows, buttons, etc.; coverall aprons; beach robes made from towels; children's pinafores; baby bibs, gowns, shirts, etc.; Bible and book covers; bookmarks.

For instructions, patterns, and more ideas, do research in your library, bookstores, and stores where crafts are sold.

Related fundraising ideas: Crafts Home Parties; Custom Crafts Shop
Success story: Strawberry Festival
Resources: American School of Needlework; Annie's Attic, Inc.; Chartwell Books; Chilton Book Company; Crafts 'N Things; Dover Publications, Inc.; Mallard Press; McCall Pattern Co.; Meredith Press Corporation; Smithmark Publishers Inc.; Sterling Publishing Co., Inc.; The DMC Corporation; Trafalgar Square Publishing; Workbasket Magazine

CRAFTS HOME PARTIES

Hold a series of home parties. Various hostesses invite friends, serve refreshments, and later deliver orders. At the parties, a member of your group leads games, gives away door prizes, displays sample merchandise and takes orders for items.

The merchandise samples consist of craft items that can be ordered for delivery in three weeks. The sample crafts are supplied by the person(s) willing to make the crafts to fill the orders. With the sample items might be samples of other materials the item can be made from or pictures of the item in a different form or size, or with various modifications.

Be alert to negotiate a later delivery date if one item receives too many orders to be filled in three weeks. Customers should complete a form specifying what is being ordered and pay a nonrefundable down payment. Request a phone number in case more information is needed or a problem develops. It would be ideal to have the people who will make the merchandise present so they can talk directly to those ordering.

An alternative to the home party scenario is to have a large scale party in a hall and have all members of the group raising funds to invite friends to accompany them. Designated hostesses will be responsible for delivering merchandise and collecting the balance of the price.

Related fundraising ideas: Crafts Booth; Custom Crafts Shop

CUSTOM CRAFTS SHOP

Make arrangements with a small shop, beauty shop, or other appropriate business to operate a custom made crafts corner. They can operate it for you as a community service or receive a modest commission for their help.

Samples of items which require many hours of work, such as quilts, afghans, hooked rugs, knit sweaters, hand-painted cards, furniture, etc., are displayed with descriptions and perhaps pictures of variations available. With each item is a specialized order form to be completed. The order form indicates prices, the nonrefundable deposit needed, the delivery time required and any other information needed by the crafts person offering the item.

Someone qualified to answer questions for potential customers should be available at the display site and should have the phone numbers of members of the group who are coordinating the fundraising project. In addition to handling inquiries, the group's committee takes care of advertising, attractively displaying items which can be ordered, and maintaining a supply of order forms. The funds raised can be from commissions for orders or from a fee charged each craftsperson for the display and order service.

Related fundraising ideas: Crafts Booth; Crafts Home Parties

DANCE EXHIBITION AND CONTEST

Enlist a ballroom dancing teacher, dance studio owner, dancing club, or ballroom operator to sponsor a couples dance exhibition and contest. The types of dance could be of one variety or several; the rules simple or complex; the prizes inexpensive or grand enough to charge a significant entrance fee. With the right location the exhibition and or contest could be the entertainment for a dinner or dance.

DANCES

A dance to raise money can range from a casual-dress affair with music from a stereo to a formal ball with a well-known band. A dance requires customers who like to dance, good music and some side benefits or events which add to the fun.

A dance committee chooses a date and place, decides on a theme and desired atmosphere, arranges for the music, agrees on the admission price, prints and sells tickets, prepares the chosen refreshments, and plans the schedule for the evening. If other fundraising events are to be included, it would be wise for the dance committee to enlist separate committees to be in charge of these activities under guidelines set by the dance committee. Side events might include a dance contest, prizes for costumes, raffles, etc.

Resource: STUMPS—One Party Place

DELIVERY SERVICE

Survey local businesses to see if there is a need for a delivery service. If so, volunteers can provide the service or the organization can do the organizational work and employ young people to do the deliveries.

DEMONSTRATION MEALS

Sell tickets to a meal that includes a cooking demonstration. The demonstration can be for one or more of the foods which are part of the meal. Examples of the type of demonstrations which might appeal to cooks are wok stir fry dishes, hot hors d'oeuvres, breads, pasta, sauces, meal in a microwave, cake decorating, ethnic dishes, sugar-free desserts, and vegetarian dishes. Recipes and printed instructions should be available. The person demonstrating must be knowledgeable and personable. A hostess should be designated to keep things running smoothly. Numbers will be limited, so ticket prices should reflect the small size of the group.

DEMONSTRATIONS

Gather in one place organizations and businesses which can provide a demonstration of some kind to help them promote their product, service or cause. The demonstrators can also sell products and give out literature, but a pertinent demonstration is a condition for participation. The following are examples of those who might choose to participate: makers of crafts could demonstrate the making of one of the products they sell; a karate teacher could demonstrate the basics of self defense; the Red Cross could demonstrate artificial respiration on a teaching mannequin and advertise classes and other services; a square dance club could demonstrate and promote beginner lessons; an accessories shop could demonstrate scarf tying; a beauty shop could offer hair styling for a randomly selected observer; a cosmetics salesperson could demonstrate makeup techniques; a sporting goods store could demonstrate proper golf swings or tennis strokes; a gym could have a teacher and pupils demonstrating an aerobics class or exercises with weights; a literacy program could demonstrate their teacher training techniques; a country and western club could teach simple line dancing steps. The possibilities are many. The group would make money from fees from the demonstrators, a modest admission charge, and the ever needed food for sale.

DINNER DELIVERED

Offer a complete home cooked meal delivered. Target busy homemakers and bachelors for the advertising. Few organizations and volunteers could sustain this fundraiser on a regular basis, but consider making the offer for Friday nights, Saturday nights, or weekend nights once a month. If the price is right, a team of workers may offer traditional Thanksgiving or Christmas dinners to be delivered. Other specialty dinners might include candles and flowers with a dinner for two, dinner for the health conscious (especially low calorie), and homemade TV dinners for those confined to home. Members could donate their specialty dishes and the basics could be cooked in a central location. Some items may be prepared in advance and be frozen for a short period of time.

Related fundraising ideas: Breakfast in Bed—Delivered; Lunch Delivered/Packed

DIRECTORIES

If your group has workers willing to produce the information for a directory, or if you are willing to hire someone to do this work, there are several options. The following are examples of directories you might produce for sale in your community: Sites of Interest to Visitors; Church Directory, with helpful information about each church; Membership Directory for one church; Antique Shop and Dealer Directory, listing all within an hour's drive; School Directory, listing names, addresses, and phone numbers of all children in a specific school; Medical Services Directory, including staff credentials, specialties, and office hours as well as addresses and telephone numbers. You would, of course, obtain written permission from the people listed to use their names in the directory.

Businesses and organizations will probably be interested in buying an advertisement in a local directory. This will be a major source of income. Enough advertisement could allow distribution of the directory free.

Related fundraising idea: Ad Space

DIRECTORY FOR BABYSITTING

Compile and sell a babysitting directory. Charge babysitters for being listed in the directory. Sell ads to appropriate businesses. Sell the directories to parents who use babysitting services.

Each babysitter's entry should include the names and phone numbers of references. Be sure to specify that your directory only indicates that the people listed are available for work, and that you have not investigated or certified their qualifications. Include a tear-out sheet for the parents to use to indicate emergency phone numbers and any special instructions needed by the baby-sitter.

If the directory earns sufficient funds, enter the entries on a computer disk and update the directory yearly. It might be expanded and include sections for yard workers, house cleaners, pet sitters, house sitters, etc.

Related fundraising idea: Ad Space

DIVORCED FATHERS SERVICE

Some divorced fathers have a difficult time remembering to provide cards and gifts for their children on birthdays, Christmas, etc. Others can re-member the occasion but have a difficult time selecting the gifts. Offer a shopping service and, if needed, a delivery or mailing service. The charge would be the cost of the gift, wrapping supplies, and postage plus the service fee for the time of the worker; the service fee is donated to the worthy cause. The volunteer shopper can make individual arrangements with the father. The gifts can be in a designated price range and the father can complete a questionnaire which will provide some guidance for the shopper. At the time the package is given to or mailed for the father, he would receive a description of the gift provided. This fundraising service may be seen by some volunteers as a worthy cause in itself if they have had experience with disappointment in a child of divorced parents.

DOOR TO DOOR

Children's groups, supervised by adults, seem best for this ingenious fundraising idea. A carefully coached child knocks on a door, explains that he or she is helping raise money for the worthy cause in question, and asks if the person who answered the door would be willing to donate one item (such as an egg, a potato, or a can of food) to benefit the cause. The child accepts the item that is given, goes next door and tells the person who answers the door that he or she is helping raise money for the worthy cause. The child then displays the item the person next door just donated and asks for a donation (any amount) in exchange for the item. This process is repeated until the workers are tired. Note that no capital is required for this project; all money collected is clear profit. The adults who are with the children should be close enough to answer questions, encourage the children if they are not successful with every person, and take care of any problems.

DRESS DOWN FOR CHARITY

In businesses and agencies where the normal dress is suit and tie for men and high heels and nylons for women, a "dress down for charity" can be an easy and successful fundraising project. The manager or owner gives his or her blessing for the members of a company, agency, department or some other division of workers to work one or more specified days in their casual clothes which would not normally be worn to work. In return for this privilege, the worker donates a specified amount of money for the charity. If customers or the public will be interacting with the "dressed down" workers, a large poster can proclaim that they are taking part in a campaign to raise money for a good cause.

EARLY AMERICAN THEME

This theme is very broad. A group could center in on one of several variations or hold several related events each featuring a different early American time. Thanksgiving time could bring to mind the first settlers. Christmas time might feature Colonial days. July 4 would call to mind the Revolutionary War period. The pioneers going west could inspire a theme. Or a theme could feature Indians and their way of life.

Patriotic items, a red, white and blue color scheme, and music would be appropriate for most early American periods. Clothing styles for all periods and themes would be interesting and lend atmosphere. Cured ham, dried fruits, baked beans, pumpkin pies, bread pudding, and sweet cider are examples of foods which support this theme.

Resource: Dover Publications, Inc.

ELECTIONS FOR A SPECIAL OFFICE

Create a special office or title and hold a mock election. Have candidates pay or have their campaign committees pay to get onto the ballot and voters pay for the privilege of voting—all for a good cause. Perhaps a neighborhood needs an Honorary Mayor. A mock election could select the Sexiest Man in Town, the Ugliest Man in the Club, the World's Worst Cook; Champion (or Worst) Joke Teller; Best Neighbor; Best Penny Pincher—the possibilities are endless.

Look for candidates who are well known and like to have fun. Stage campaign kickoff speeches after candidates are selected and don't forget the victory party with voting continuing until near the end of the party when the winner gives his/her acceptance speech.

Success story: Mock Election

ENTREPRENEUR COMPETITION

Enlist individuals, partners, couples, families, teams or some other type of groups—the more the better—to enter an entrepreneur competition. Give each person or group the same amount of capital (perhaps $20) and a length of time (perhaps 3 to 6 months) and allow them to see how much money they can raise for the good cause while adding only labor and or donated services of others to their capital.

Have a concluding event where the competitors bring in their earnings and a brief report on how they earned their profit. Recognition should be given to all who participate, and you should add something special for the most successful entrepreneurs. A seat at a head table, a corsage or boutonniere, or their picture on a "Wall of Fame" are examples of inexpensive way to provide recognition.

EXERCISE CLUB

If you have access to an appropriate location, you might be able to offer a membership-owned health club for a reasonable cost. You could seek donations of unused weights, exercise bicycles, a TV and VCR and exercise tapes. Volunteers could keep the place organized and clean and schedule exercise sessions led by the videotapes at specific times.

This project would require injury releases from the participants and guidelines for use of the facilities. Legal advice would be in order.

EXHIBITION GAMES

Sports fans will pay to see almost any team sport. A professional game to benefit charity is a possibility, but organizers can also approach area high school, college, and community league officials and coaches. Although team sports are popular, also consider a tennis match, golf event, or bowling tournament. If you can get celebrities involved, you'll attract more publicity and sell more tickets. Sports figures may be willing to play a sport other than their major one off season. The mayor, football coach, pastor of the largest church in town, 20-year senior class sponsor and other well-known locals playing a sport will sell tickets.

Income will come from ticket sales, program advertisements, souvenirs, food sales, and things like raffles tied in with the exhibition game.

FAIRS

Fair, festival, bazaar and carnival are all terms used broadly by fundraising groups to represent an event which features a variety of entertainments and items for sale to benefit a worthy cause. Ideas for organizing exhibitions and displays are presented in this section. See **Bazaars** if you need ideas for merchandise to sell as part of your fair. If you are considering having games, side shows, or rides, see **Carnivals** for suggestions. Performance possibilities are discussed in the **Festivals** entry.

Exhibitions and displays can be assembled for a wide variety of items. Sometimes they are competitive, with some type of award offered to exhibitors. Some displays are primarily educational. Businesses and institutions provide exhibits for promotion of goods and services or to build goodwill. All exhibitions and displays must be of interest to a significant number of people in order to be useful for fundraising. Consider combining the exhibitions with some other related event. The theme and or occasions for your fair will dictate the type of displays.

A committee familiar with the possible participants and customers must make an informed decision about what type of exhibition or display to feature. The following categories of items are possibilities: antique items (farm tools, kitchen items, clothing, dishes, needlework, jewelry, etc.); quilts; needlework; fashions (display or show, current or period styles); dolls, doll houses, and doll furniture; collections (cups and saucers, spoons, stamps, coins, bottles, etc.); model cars, trains, and ships; flower arrangements; photographs of a particular type of subject (children, local buildings, scenery, prom or wedding pictures of local residents, etc.); plants (violets, cacti, etc.); displays related to fishing, golf, tennis, or other professional sports.

If you have competitions as part of your exhibition, be sure you give all concerned a written statement of how the items will be judged and the awards or prizes which are offered. Choose impartial, knowledgeable judges and involve them in setting the criteria and guidelines prior to advertising the event.

Related fundraising ideas: Antique Show; Art Show; Demonstrations; Needlework Shop
Success story: Quilt Show

FAMILY FEUD

Have a program which is a parody of the *Family Feud* television game show. The contestants can be groups of family members or groups representing high school classes or businesses or agencies. Keep the questions secret and the process and rules strictly on the "up and up" with respected judges on hand. Do, however, have a prep session during which the contestants can practice sessions and develop some dramatic style which will be entertaining to the audience.

Other current and older television shows can stimulate ideas for entertaining skits or show segments. For the shows which feature celebrity contestants, enlist a volunteer to play the part of a celebrity with a distinctive voice, clothing, saying, or style. Michael Jackson, Madonna, Elizabeth Taylor, Willie Nelson, Dolly Parton, Elvis Presley, and a *Star Trek* character are but a few examples. Look at the people available to you and see if any of them can call to mind a celebrity they can portray.

FASHION SHOWS

Fashion shows come in many varieties, but all have some elements in common. The main ingredients are interesting clothing to model, suitable models, and a commentator with an appropriate script describing the fashions. A theme narrows the group's choices in terms of type of clothing, appropriate models, audience appeal, decorations, and complementary activities. A location must provide a runway area of some type, adequate lighting (including a spotlight if possible), a speaker's stand and sound system, dressing rooms for the models, hanging and organizing space for the fashions, and seats for the desired number of ticket holders. Volunteer workers, publicity, tickets, music, door prizes, programs, decorations, and food are other key elements.

Dress shop owners and fashion coordinators of clothing departments are common sources of fashions to model. The committee may make arrangements to borrow fashions from several stores that feature different types of clothing. Some fashion shows feature clothing made by individuals in the community or members of a high school home economics class. Period clothing owned by members of the community can play a key role in fashion shows with appropriate themes.

Models are sometimes supplied with the fashions, but usually they are enlisted by the group sponsoring the show. Group members and family members and friends often serve as models, and their participation will boost ticket sales.

An experienced commentator is an asset. Consider enlisting a local television or radio announcer. Any adult with a good voice and stage presence can fill this role if he or she has a good script. The script should be written by the professionals who provide the fashions if possible; if they are not available, select a writer from your group who is knowledgeable about clothing and fashion. Scripts should be written in large print; having each garment described on a separate card or sheet of paper allows changes at the last minute.

Themes for fashion shows can be anything that will attract the desired audience. A variety of the latest fashions, wedding fashions (old or new), antique clothing, handmade fashions, children's clothing, vacation clothing, clothing with ethnic influences, fashion contrasts through the years, and an Easter parade are examples to stimulate your thinking.

The location will determine the number of tickets you can sell. You may well want to have a fashion show in a restaurant or hall in connection with a brunch, lunch, tea, or dinner. Another choice is a larger theater type area with a stage. Wherever the show is held, create a floorplan which includes a designated place for every activity. The dressing room, model entrance point, "runway" walk, exit point, location of commentator, and location of musicians (if any are used) need special consideration. Walk through your planned setup before everyone arrives for rehearsal.

Music can be live in the form of an organist, pianist, string trio, etc. or recorded music. It should be soft during the fashion presentation so it will not compete with the commentator.

Publicity and programs must give credit to all businesses and organizations that have provided the organizers with assistance. Programs may include sold advertisements. Door prizes should be donated or made by group members.

Food, door prizes, exhibits by businesses related to the theme (such as photographers, and florists for a wedding fashion show), and other activities not directly related to the fashion presentations should have committees that are free to concentrate on these areas during the show.

The planners should keep the fashion show to a reasonable length. An hour is not too short; two hours is probably too long. Keep things moving at a steady pace to prevent audience restlessness.

Some department stores designate part of their advertising budget for fashion shows featuring a particular brand of clothing to benefit a charitable organization. This is an easier route for a group desiring to raise funds with a fashion show; the main challenge then becomes advertising the show and selling an adequate number of tickets.

Success story: A Family Fashion Show

FESTIVALS

Festival, fair, bazaar, and carnival are all terms used broadly by fundraising groups to represent an event which features a variety of entertainments and items for sale to benefit a worthy cause. Performance possibilities are presented in this section. Ideas for organizing exhibitions and displays are discussed under **Fairs**. The section on **Bazaars** emphasizes the sale of all manner of merchandise. The **Carnivals** section indicates games, side shows, and rides to consider.

By definition, a festival is a celebration of a specific type which offers entertainment or a series of performances of a certain kind. While sales of food and articles may take place at a festival, entertainment is the chief focus. Festivals may be entertainments of a special category, such as an art festival, dance festival, drama festival, or music festival. Sometimes a variety of entertainments is collected and called an arts festival.

Indicated below are examples of possible performances which could be part of a festival.

- **Art** (painting, sculpture, photographs, crafts, etc.): indoor and or outdoor exhibits; tours of museums or artists' studios; demonstrations by artists; illustrated lectures on an art related topic.
- **Dance** (tap, ballet, modern, square dance, imperial, ethnic of all kinds, etc.): performances by individuals, partners, small groups, dance classes, pom pom school groups.
- **Drama**: play (school or community drama group); movie (classic or new); musical; pageant; story-telling; famous speeches; poetry reading; melodrama (cheer the hero, hiss the villain); murder mystery theater.
- **Music** (concerts or assorted selections by individuals or groups): bands, orchestras, brass or strings ensembles; jazz; glee clubs; gospel choirs; folk singers; country and western; bluegrass, etc. Music lends itself to any theme or event.

A festival must be planned around the talent available to the group. However, it is a rare group which does not have access to artists and performers. Consult school, community and church leaders for ideas. Talk to businesses that deal in arts related products. Check your telephone directory and advertisements in the local newspaper. Some professionals just getting started will do benefits free or for expenses. A location for performances may come with your artists and performers. You can seek the use of a public building and grounds, such as school facilities, parks, government buildings and grounds.

Center in on the type of festival which is most appropriate for your group and then enlist committee members who have some expertise needed for the event. Remember that the committee will need members with organizational, financial, and merchandising skills as well as those familiar with the arts.

Related fundraising ideas: Concerts; Fashion Shows; Melodrama; Murder Mystery Dinner Theater; Professional Entertainment; Shows for Kids; Strolling Musicians; Talent Show; Theater Party.

FIREWOOD SALES

If the group has a supply of firewood available, customers who will pay them profitably for delivered firewood, a truck or trailer, and willing workers, this is a good seasonal fundraising idea. Firewood sales are especially good for men's organizations. Under some circumstances, the group can cut the firewood. This requires extra considerations in regard to tools and safety.

FISH FRY

Some organizations have regularly scheduled fish fries and develop a regular clientele. Customers usually expect fried potatoes and perhaps hushpuppies with their fish. It is a good idea to also offer hot dogs or spaghetti for family members who do not eat fish. Experienced cooks who are willing to produce individual pieces of fish cooked to perfection are needed for this fundraiser. Members of the group frequently donate slaw, desserts and other foods for the fish fry meals.

FLEA MARKET

Organize a flea market and lease stalls to individuals and other groups. You can, of course, operate some of the stalls for your organization. By all means control the food sales. Not only will the customers want to buy refreshments, but you should also have a brisk business selling and delivering to the people who are selling their wares.

Flea markets can be regular weekend events or held only once for a few days, probably a weekend. Spring and fall are favorite flea market times. Markets are set up in large areas—such as a school gym, a parking lot, along both sides of a street, a park, a drive-in theater, a local farmer's market, or an empty store. The organization can provide tables or require the sellers to provide their own tables and display racks.

If there are established flea markets in your area, your group could investigate operating a stall at some other group's market.

Success story: Flea Market and Auction

FLEA MARKET BOOTH

In this booth you sell anything that is secondhand. Exclude clothing if you have a special boutique booth. Except for antiques, price everything low so it will sell.

A pickup service will increase the items donated for this booth. It is also important to collect items over a long period of time and store them until the sale. Most people discard useable items on their personal schedule and appreciate recipients who make it convenient for them.

You will need a lot of setup help. Items should all be in working order— test them. Clean things that are dirty. Remove items from containers that are worn or torn. Have sacks, boxes, and newspapers for packing. Attach prices that are easy to remove and have designated volunteers with change available to collect the money and package the items. Those in charge of the money need a table at the entrance and exit of the booth.

A flea market booth can stock anything. Dishes, knickknacks, bottles, candlesticks, lamps, jewelry, flower arrangements, decorations, and appliances that work are just some of the possibilities.

Success story: Flea Market and Auction

FOOD—BUSINESS CATERING

Invite businesses to bring their breakfast meetings to your dining hall; prepare and deliver delicious box lunches to the business; obtain permission to sell "coffee break" food and beverages at a specific time period on a regular schedule; arrange to run a concession during a business conference or convention. Think like a business person seeking to make a profit providing food and then organize your group to raise funds. This will work much more smoothly if you offer a service that is not already being offered rather than competing.

FOOD—CONCESSIONS

Seek permission from a school or community league to operate food concessions at sporting events. Or set up refreshment stands in public parks during heavy traffic times. Offer simple food from a van or truck as workers arrive at and leave a large company. Be sure to have signs clearly announcing that you are raising funds for a good cause and not a business.

Related fundraising ideas: Hamburger Stand; Hot Dog Stand; Popcorn
Success story: Strawberry Festival

FOOD—MEALS

Whether you are offering breakfast, brunch, lunch, supper, or dinner as a fundraising project, there are some basics to consider. Your facilities must be able to accommodate what you are planning. The food should either be easy to prepare or be of the type that can be prepared ahead without losing quality. Be sure foods designed to be hot are served hot and cold foods arrive to the customers cold. The serving and eating areas should remain clean and as attractive as possible, so you should assign workers to clean constantly and provide plenty of trash containers.

Plan ahead the way your food will be arranged, prepared, and served. Someone should be designated to serve as host and troubleshooter. If everyone is working at a task, no one is observing the whole picture and spotting problems.

How much of the food and ingredients are donated and what happens to the leftovers will have an impact on the profits from the meals prepared. The people in charge must practice both profit and quality control to be successful.

Related fundraising ideas: Breakfast in Bed—Delivered; Chili Cook-off Dinner; Demonstration Meals; Dinner Delivered; Fish Fry; Food—Smorgasbord; Hot Dog and Marshmallow Roast; Lunch Delivered/Packed; Pancake Breakfast; Progressive Supper; Salad Luncheon; Spaghetti Supper.
Success stories: Brunch and Speaker; Dinner Theater Production; Field Party
Resource: Outlet Book Company, Inc.

FOOD—SMORGASBORD

A smorgasbord fundraiser has many advantages. Everyone expects to find several things they like among the offerings. Those who like the "all you can eat" concept will be attracted. A smorgasbord lends itself well to having many workers provide their special dishes for the table.

A smorgasbord can be offered for breakfast, brunch, lunch, afternoon tea, dinner, or midnight supper. A selection of appetizer type foods are popular with many people—meatballs, small hot dogs in sauce, egg rolls, ravioli, chicken wings, quiche, vegetable pieces and dip, fruit and chocolate sauce, etc.

FOOD BOOTH

In deciding what food to sell, consider the facilities you will have available and the theme of your event. A major consideration is also how much money you will make on each item. Keep the food as simple as possible, limit the choices in any category, and have plenty of napkins, plastic utensils, paper plates, and waste containers available.

If you have a kitchen available, the possibilities are limited only by your equipment and space needs. You can serve whole dinners or items like chili, tacos, enchiladas, pizza, hamburgers, hot dogs, corn on the cob, melted cheese on chips, hot soft pretzels, and ice cream sandwiches. Morning time lends itself to cinnamon rolls, muffins, doughnuts, bagels and cream cheese, hot biscuits, corn muffins or even fresh pancakes and waffles. If electricity is available, but not a kitchen, you can serve items cooked in electric skillets or crock pots or microwaves or roasters. A coffee pot can provide coffee, hot cider, and hot chocolate. An ice chest allows sandwiches and sodas. Brownies, candy, popcorn and chips can be sold anywhere.

At the cash register you might offer baked items, jelly, jam, homemade spaghetti sauce, hot mustard or other specialty items. Don't overlook any possibility of having food items donated or fixed at home and delivered ready to serve.

Resource: Smithmark Publishers

FORTUNES

Fortune tellers with crystal balls, gypsies who read palms or tea leaves, horoscope casters, card readers, and other dramatic occultists can provide good entertainment value for the money they charge customers. Volunteers who accept this project can collect sample fortunes, predictions, and instruction books on the subject. A costume, even if it is only dramatic clothing, is a must and the atmosphere where the fortunes are told should be as interesting as possible. A tent made colorful or an isolated corner table at a gathering or inside a van with chairs at a table are examples; use imagination and a sense of the mysterious. The fortune teller needs an assistant with an attitude and costume that add to the fun. The person greeting customers and taking money should have prepared several colorful tales of the wonderful things that the fortune teller foretold for past customers.

Resources: Enslow Publishers, Inc.; Prentice Hall General Reference

FOURTH OF JULY THEME

All things red, white and blue and patriotic are appropriate for a Fourth of July theme. The week of July 4 is dictated, if not the actual date. A fireworks display is expected. If your area, or a town within a comfortable driving distance, has a traditional fireworks display, your group might arrange a special location or service related to their event. If the planners act early, you might be able to have a reception in a hotel room or business conference room which provides a good view of the fireworks.

A picnic with competitive games and tournaments would attract families. Set up three-legged races, a raw-egg toss, horseshoe tournaments or even things like checker tournaments for those who like to relax in the shade. Award small flags to winners. Raffle a large ice cooler or two nice lounge chairs. Sell snow cones with red and blue syrup. Arrange for a band and singers to provide classic patriotic music. Hold Mr. and Ms. U.S.A. costume contests. Pit the firemen against the policemen in a tug of war. Hold a parade of children on tricycles and bicycles decorated in red, white and blue. Hold a mock campaign speech contest for some local office with awards for the funniest, the most believable, etc.; let the person holding that office award the prizes.

Resource: Contemporary Drama Service

FRUIT BASKETS

Make up order forms which specify the contents, delivery dates, prices, and required deposit for three of four types of fruit baskets. Give each sales person a photograph of sample baskets made by the committee which will prepare the ordered baskets. Be sure you have a reliable source for the baskets, the fruit offered, and the packing supplies needed. Take the orders and then form committees to create and deliver the baskets.

GARAGE SALE

A group can advantageously schedule a series of two, three, or four garage sales over a period of a few months. The sales can be held at the homes of members who live in different areas of town. This allows for collecting items for all the sales in the same campaign. Advertise all the sales, providing customers a choice of dates and locations, and move items left from the earlier sales to the later sales with lower prices.

All sale items should be clean and displayed as attractively as possible. Tables can be covered with sheets which provide overhang to hide boxes and other containers from sight. Tables can be made from doors or boards placed across two sawhorses.

Shelves can be fashioned from boards placed on the steps of two matching ladders. Pegboards and hooks are convenient for displaying some items. If you are selling many clothes, provide a mirror and screens for a dressing room.

In addition to prior newspaper and radio announcements and flyers, place sale signs in the neighborhood for each sale. Make the signs as attractive as possible to encourage the idea that you will have quality items.

Where you specify the time of the sale, indicate that items will be drastically reduced for the last hour. It is also a good idea to indicate that there will be no "early sales" and to follow that policy. Don't forget to take down the signs after your sale.

Related fundraising ideas: Rummage Sale; Flea Market; Thrift Shops

GENEALOGY WORKSHOPS

There is sufficient interest in genealogy to explore offering workshops to assist those who desire help in researching their family trees. Look for a leader who is knowledgeable in the process and enthusiastic about helping others.

Decide on the number of people who will allow both an acceptable profit and individual help and set the charge accordingly. If the interest is higher than the number appropriate for one workshop, by all means schedule other sessions.

Resource: The Everton Publishers

GIFT WRAPPING SERVICE

Whenever you sell anything that is likely to be purchased as a gift, offer a gift wrapping service. Have appropriate supplies and a wrapper who enjoys this type of work. Try to get the wrapping supplies donated or sold to you for wholesale prices. Charge enough to make a profit. Your best advertising will be signs and the suggestions of salespeople where the items are purchased.

Related fundraising idea: Christmas Gift Wrapping Booth
Resources: Chilton Book Company; Crown Publishers, Inc.; Leisure Arts

GOLF SCRAMBLE

Hold a golf tournament that is a four-person scramble. After each round, the team determines the best position obtained by one of its four players and all then play from that position. The winners receive donated prizes. The tickets are priced to more than cover expenses, and the profit goes to the designated cause. This is a suitable event for businesses to sponsor a team of their employees. Often a luncheon or dinner is provided for participants.

GOOD OLE DAYS THEME

A good approach to this theme is to celebrate a particular decade or have sections or events to celebrate several decades. Whether the group chooses the '20s, '30s, '40s, '50s, '60s or any other decade, they can find song collections from that era and identify distinctive clothing styles, fads, celebrities, and significant historical events. This theme provides especially good entertainment possibilities. Each period produced classic movies, well-known performers, and favorite songs and dances.

Related fundraising ideas: Early American Theme; Melodrama; Pictures with Impersonators;
   Pie Supper; Victorian Booth
Resources: Dover Publications, Inc.; Music Dispatch; Plays, Inc., Publishers

GRAB BAGS

Collect from businesses and individuals new or secondhand items in excellent condition, wrap them and place them in a grab bag. Indicate the range of value of the items in the bag, state that some of the packages include cash which is at least twice the cost to participate, and charge a set price to select an item. This will appeal to the gambling instincts of those predisposed to support your good cause.

This idea is comparatively easy and can be operated at any large meeting or an event where a number of people are present. Leftover items can be included in your next grab bag project.

GRANDPARENT & GRANDCHILDREN EVENTS

Organizing outings designed for grandparents and grandchildren will attract customers in many communities, if advertised properly. The people in charge of the events can act as tour guides. They make all the arrangements, go along to keep everything on scheule, and take care of transportation, tickets, and problems. This leaves the grandparents free to enjoy their grandchildren.

The events can vary greatly. Examples are a picnic with food and games, a trip to a zoo in a nearby town, a magic show, a day at a carnival or fair, a crafts make-and-take event, a hay ride, a special movie showing, lunch out and a movie, and a tour of a historical site or museum.

HALLOWEEN EVENTS

Halloween offers a variety of opportunities for fundraising. A group can offer pumpkins and jack-o'-lanterns for sale in a shopping center. Sell yard decorations consisting of a bale of hay, stalks of corn, pumpkins, and a scarecrow; include removal service in the fee charged. Have a costume party and contest for children, adults, or families. Fill a hall with carnival type games for children and make sure all win candy and small prizes; parents buy tickets at a central booth. Rent workers to be witches, goblins, ghosts, monsters, etc., to visit Halloween parties to talk to the guests and pose for pictures. Sponsor an all-night family party in the local school gym with active games early in the evening, ghost stories with a midnight supper, and movies for the early morning; end with breakfast.

Hay rides and campfire events are good for this time of the year, if the weather cooperates. There is a Halloween fundraiser appropriate for most groups.

Related fundraising ideas: Balloons—Helium; Caramel Apples & Popcorn Balls; Fortunes; Haunted House; Hay Rides; Hot Dog and Marshmallow Roast; Murder Mystery Dinner Theater; Mystery Trips; Pumpkins Painted; Treasure Hunt.
Resource: Special Music Company and Pair Records; STUMPS—One Party Place; The H.W. Wilson Company

HAMBURGER STAND

When operating a hamburger stand or selling hamburgers as part of a meal, it is important that you protect the meat from deterioration. Rather thin hamburger patties can be prepared in advance, stacked with wax paper between them and frozen until time to begin cooking them for sale. Offer salad dressing, mustard, and catsup as well as pickles, onions, and lettuce as toppings. Hamburgers barbecued on a grill should sell well when the weather is nice.

Drinks are a must at a hamburger stand, and french fries or chips are expected.

HARVEST BOOTH

At a fall event, a harvest booth offers a variety of possibilities. Decorations and items for sale can be items we associate with Halloween and Thanksgiving or foods being harvested.

Consider the following list: Halloween decorations, favors for trick-or-treaters, fall flowers in arrangements, Thanksgiving decorations and centerpieces, pumpkins and pumpkins with painted faces, scarecrows, shocks of corn, squash, cornucopia decorations, food (featuring pies, breads, cookies, jams, jellies, and butters made of pumpkin, squash, apples, peaches, etc.), sweatshirts decorated for the fall holidays or in fall colors, and ceramic containers or figurines which fit the theme. Think fall holidays and fall colors and your ideas will fit in a harvest booth.

HATTERS

Hatters offer for sale one special hat style or hats of all kinds. A hatter will have hats appropriate for the season and theme. The hats can be sold from a booth with roving salespeople wearing a hat and carrying others to attract attention to the booth. Don't forget mirrors, so customers will be able to model the hats for themselves. During hot weather, hats that provide shade will be popular merchandise at many events.

HAUNTED HOUSE

A haunted house makes a fun project but takes a great deal of effort to arrange, especially the first time. An empty old house is a wonderful site but probably hard to locate. You might check with some real estate agents to see if they have an empty house that could be rented from the owner for a few weeks. Other possibilities are empty stores, basements, sections of schools or churches, a large garage, or a barn. Look with a creative eye for a place you can transform into a spooky place. When you decide on a site, *be sure there are no safety hazards* that could contribute to hurting anyone involved. Decide on the best entrance, route, and exit for the paying customers, then devise the scary effects.

Have a brainstorming session to gather ideas for costumes, sounds, weird noises, lighting effects, etc. If someone in a town nearby operates a haunted house, see if they will advise you as a courtesy or for a modest fee. Flashing a light on a corpse or mummy rising from a coffin, a witch stirring and casting spells over a kettle, a cold or warm wind blowing across the faces, rats and bats made from black fake fur, garden hose snakes, vampire or zombie scenes, an empty chair rocking, scary monster masks, tombstones with epitaphs, and moving skeleton figures are some ideas. A section can feature a witch allowing customers to feel eyes (grapes), brains (spaghetti), hands (stuffed rubber gloves), teeth (large kernels of corn), ears (dried apricots), liver or heart (made from *very* firm gelatin), noses (ends of hot dogs) and other body parts which have been preserved in bowls. Sheets can form ghosts which float free from the ceiling; paint and cloth which glow in the dark can create spooky sights. Covers over end-to-end sturdy tables can create a cave entrance or exit or a side trip into a tomb. Buy a flasher button and use colored bulbs in lamps and other light fixtures.

Have an abundance of responsible, alert adults working at all times to be sure things run smoothly and safely. The guides through the house can do much to add to the feeling of excitement by what they say and do: share everyone's best "sick" jokes and stories for all workers to use.

A shop at a haunted house could sell masks, fake blood, makeup, false scars and scabs, creepy spiders, snakes, bats, ghost mobiles, appropriate printed helium balloons, haunted-design shirts, trick-or-treat toys and candy, etc. Food for sale could be simple and standard fare or creative with a look or name that supports the haunted house and Halloween theme.

Resources: Baker's Plays; Lonestar Technologies, Ltd.; Special Music Company and Pair Records

HAWAIIAN THEME

This theme seems to ask for warm weather and blue skies and workers in bright clothes or grass skirts and leis. Decorations and products would tend toward beach and warm weather items. Foods would be luau style featuring roast pork, rice dishes and pineapple, mangoes and other tropical fruits. Outside booths to sell all kinds of products while Hawaiian music and hula dancers provided atmosphere would be ideal.

Resources: Barnes & Noble; St. Louis Carnival Supply; STUMPS—One Party Place

HAY RIDES

Some businesses provide hay rides, and it might be possible to use their facilities and share the profits. A better idea would be to locate someone with a farm, wagon, hay and tractor who would donate the use of these things to benefit your good cause.

Provide a campfire, a hot dog and marshmallow roast, and some music at the middle or end of the ride. If you do this around Halloween, ghost stories would be in order. A Fourth of July ride could end with fireworks.

The hay ride will make more money if the wagon makes several round trips and there is food and entertainment at both the beginning point and the destination.

Related fundraising idea: Hot Dog and Marshmallow Roast

HERBS AND SPICES BOOTH

A booth featuring herbs works best if you have volunteers who are knowledgeable about herbs—especially if they grow them and can donate dried herbs. Another possibility is for someone who is interested in herbs to locate a good wholesale supply and then package the herbs in some attractive way.

Items for sale could include various potpourri and potpourri sachets and hot pads; dried herbs and spices in attractive packages or containers; catnip toys; pomander balls; vinegar with herbs; herb jellies; herb butters; racks to dry herbs; miniature herb gardens, with instructions for care attached; potted herbs; potting soil; bath herbs tied in cheesecloth; moth bags; sachets; chili sauce; spaghetti sauce; pickles; candied fruits; relishes; homemade mustards; and salad dressings.

A refrigerator or cooler may be required for some of the foods.

Resources: Dover Publications, Inc.; Smithmark Publishers Inc.

HOBBIES BOOTH

Think about the things people buy to utilize in a leisure activity and things which are associated with a hobby.

This booth might offer collectibles—preferably donated—in one section. Things like salt and pepper shakers, cups and saucers, baseball cards, thimbles, and old glass bottles are perfect. Towels, caps, shirts, and signs can be made with decorations and sayings related to a hobby. For example, small towels can be decorated with a tennis racket, golf ball, or bowling ball. See the **Personalized Booth** section for sayings which can be used on signs, shirts, caps, etc.

Craft kits with instructions would appeal to some. Ideas include a kit with the material needed and pattern for a quilt block cushion or quilt top; thread and instructions for a crocheted baby quilt; materials and pattern for a baby bib or blanket; or a wooden box ready to be decorated with a design.

Books on hobby related subjects are plentiful. Booklets, perhaps written by a volunteer, could explain how to make an item. Samples of the items described in the books and booklets could be on display or for sale. If the instructions are for a large item, supply pictures to attract interest.

Resources: Dover Publications, Inc.; The DMC Corporation

HOME INVENTORIES

Everyone needs a home inventory in case of fire or theft. If the group has volunteers who are willing to form teams to create the inventory there should be a market. The inventory can consist of a videotape with a voice description of the items being viewed. An alternative is to take photographs to be placed in a photo album. The customer can record on a tape recorder the information to accompany each picture and the workers can type the information and add it to the page with the matching picture. All valuables, such as jewelry and other valued items, can be displayed for the recording. Customers should be encouraged to create and maintain a file of purchase receipts for all items of value and those most frequently taken by thieves.

The inventory teams can practice on their own homes and the homes of other willing group members to become efficient at their task and to produce sample inventories to show potential customers.

HOME PARTIES FOR PRODUCTS

Locate a salesperson who offers home parties for an established company and then have the organization serve as host for a party.

All members can use the booklets to take orders from those who cannot come and boost sales. Negotiate for a percentage of sales; if that is not possible, take the hostess gifts and sell them at a silent auction to secure cash for the cause.

HORSE SHOWS

A horse show can be held only by those groups that have access to individuals experienced in conducting horse shows and the facilities needed for such an event. If you are located in an area where there are riding stables, riding schools, and riding clubs, consider this fundraising idea. Workers not involved with the exhibits and displays of riding skill can collect tickets, run the food stand, and perform other important tasks.

HOT DOG AND MARSHMALLOW ROAST

Build a campfire and allow the participants to roast hot dogs and marshmallows using green sticks you've cut and prepared, clothes hangers that have been straightened, or, as a last choice, long barbecue forks.

Families, fathers and sons, grandparents and

grandchildren and similar adult-children groups are good prospects for this event. Spring and fall usually offer the best weather. Remember that the weather can always require alternate plans.

This activity combines well with a nature hike, hay ride, fishing trip, or a campfire program of singing, jokes, and skits.

HOT DOG STAND

Sell hot dogs, chips, drinks and a simple dessert like cookies. Offer a collection of accompaniments: mustard (perhaps more than one kind); catsup; pickles; onions; sauerkraut; grated cheese; chili; etc. Consider turkey hot dogs for the health conscious. If you have an oven, offer hot dogs baked in biscuit or crescent roll dough. If you don't have a refrigerator, be sure to adequately prepare to keep your hot dogs and other perishable items cold in an ice chest.

HOUSE TOURS

House tours are favorite fundraisers. The organizers arrange with owners for people to tour a group of homes in a specific area. A description must be written for each home which will be visited; maps must be prepared; and tickets must be printed and sold. The literature used the day of the tour may include ads sold to businesses. Each site of the tour needs volunteers to be present in each area to provide supervision and information. Advertising is, as always, important.

Saturday and Sunday are favored tour days. The ticket price should reflect whether there is food included, the estimated number of potential customers, and the popularity of the good cause.

Older homes are traditional tour homes, but customers will also be attracted to newer homes. Some tours have featured a particular section of the homes, such as kitchens, bedrooms, patios and gardens, or guest houses. Farm houses, condos, apartments, and lakefront homes are also of interest to individuals touring; your community may offer a unique category. Never assume you cannot tour homes of interest; when you ask the owners, you may be pleasantly surprised.

Local florists may be willing to provide flowers for the homes in return for having their business cards displayed with them. The organizers of the tour will want to express their appreciation to the tour hosts, both informally and in writing, and provide them a gift in honor of their assistance.

Success story: House Tour

ICE CREAM—HOMEMADE

Homemade ice cream can be the basis for making money. Frequently individuals can furnish ice cream makers and others can supply the ingredients; otherwise the group can buy the supplies. Have toppings, cake and cookies available to eat with the ice cream and price the items to make a nice profit for the work involved. Don't forget to provide at least ice water to drink.

If you prefer, it is possible to purchase the ice cream and provide many types of toppings. You can advertise the event as an ice cream feast and serve sundaes, strawberry shortcake, banana splits, etc.

INSTRUCTION BOOKLETS

Identify something that someone knows how to do or make and that others would like to learn. Write an instruction booklet or leaflet and offer it for sale. The possible topics are endless; the important thing is to be sure the information is original and not copied from a printed source.

The instruction booklet might tell how to make a craft project which has been admired by others. You might obtain instructions for an original quilt pattern. A country line dancer might create illustrated instructions for a line dance. Advice from an experienced garage sale operator could be in demand. The possibilities are limitless.

The instructions can be printed and bound from your originals as they are sold. In addition to being sold by the members of the organization, offer the booklets through advertisements.

INTERNATIONAL THEME

An international theme is timely and fun. It takes on a special meaning if first or second generation immigrants are available to advise and participate. College students from abroad are also potential advisers and helpers. People who have traveled to other countries usually have keepsakes, they are willing to share for decorations or wear for costumes. However, an international theme can be built on research and be a learning experience for all.

The food, products, flags, dances, songs, flowers, and costumes of many countries or regions can be featured in items for sale, decorations, and entertainment. Travel posters are appropriate decorations. Enlist committees to develop sections for as many regions as possible. Your library and school geography books will be rich sources for ideas.

Resources: Barnes & Noble; Dover Publications, Inc.; NTC Publishing Group; Outlet Book Company, Inc.; Plays, Inc., Publishers

JEWELRY BOOTH

Jewelry comes in all styles and prices. Have a committee seek to obtain jewelry on consignment from a wholesaler or merchant. Keep the prices in the modest range and make the displays attractive. Handmade jewelry can be included if available. One section of the booth might offer previously owned jewelry which has been donated. Helpful and enthusiastic sales help is important.

KISSING BOOTH

A kissing booth needs to be operated in a very lighthearted and fun manner. It can be done in different ways. A customer can pay the price and then draw a slip of paper which indicates whether he or she receives a candy kiss or the choice of a kiss from one of the workers in the booth. A big ceremony could be conducted in order for candy kisses to be awarded in private and the customers enlisted to send their friends to the booth for the "wonderful" experience. A celebrity or well-known person may be willing to sell kisses for your worthy cause. Enlist the high school or college cheerleaders and football and basketball stars for sessions supplying the kisses. The persons selling kisses

might be in some kind of interesting costume. You might offer instant photographs of the event for an additional fee. The booth needs bright and colorful decorations and creative advertising.

KITCHEN BOOTH

By making or enhancing items for kitchens, you will have the core of items to sell in a booth with a kitchen theme. Possibilities include cookbooks (especially those made by the organization); recipe file cards and file boxes; home cooked items (perhaps with the recipe); decorated mugs; ceramic teapots, candy dishes, or bowls; glasses with painted designs; personalized items like Mom's Ice Cream bowl or Dad's Popcorn bowl; towels which snap or button onto towel racks; hot pads or mitts; placemat and napkin sets; napkin rings; table cloths; picnic baskets; lunchbags and boxes; hot-plate tiles or pads; aprons; barbecue aprons and hats; "Round Tuit" pot holders; place settings of dishes painted with a child-pleasing design; spices; pastry bags and tubes; brushes; cutters; wooden spoons; wire whisks; pepper mills; rolling pins and covers; chopping boards; omelet pans; ice buckets and tongs; salad servers; wall decorations; and table centerpieces.

LECTURES

Arrange for a well-known and popular speaker to give a lecture or series of lectures and sell tickets ahead of time. If you have no one in your group with a personal contact, explore using the services of a booking agency. Another possibility is to identify a subject which attracts a great deal of interest and then seek out one or a series of speakers who have expertise in the subject.

Success story: Brunch and Speaker

LUNCH DELIVERED/PACKED

Although this service might attract any working person or student, it should have special appeal for those who desire to have an appetizing lunch which meets healthful dietary standards. Customers would choose from a collection of menus appropriate for a packed lunch. The selections could include low-calorie, low-fat, salt-free, sugar-free, vegetarian, and high fiber choices as well as gourmet selections. The lunches would be prepared and delivered, or be available for pickup, at a convenient location each weekday morning. The organization could invest in carriers to maintain the temperature of cold or hot menu selections (charging a deposit for the carriers' use) or rely instead on insulated, disposable bags. Appropriate containers could be sold to customers for their convenience and your profit. If this plan is too complicated for the workers, develop customers in a large company or government building and deliver lunch one or two days a week, offering only a few—but delicious—choices.

Related fundraising ideas: Breakfast in Bed—Delivered; Dinner Delivered

MAGAZINES BOOTH

Magazines are usually discarded by their owners. Your group can collect them, offer them for sale at a flea market or other suitable places, and then dispose of those not purchased. The prices must be low, but this fundraising effort requires little or no capital. Combining magazines in a booth with books is a good idea since the two will probably appeal to the same customers.

MAKEUP BOOTH

Cosmetic companies and department stores will sometimes provide makeup sessions in return for the right to sell their products. Set up a makeup booth and provide seats and refreshments for the customers who are waiting; the group keeps the fee for the makeover and the company benefits from the makeup sold. If no company is interested in this arrangement, perhaps you have access to a qualified person who will work as a volunteer to give makeup demonstrations for a donation from the person receiving the service.

MELODRAMA

Build an evening of entertainment around a melodrama featuring members of your organization who like to act. If your group is not interested in doing the melodrama, see if you can enlist a community, school or church drama group. With the proper warmup, the audience will get into the spirit of the play and cheer the hero, hiss the villain, and "ah-h-h" for the heroine.

Supplement the melodrama with old-time spirited songs and partners telling corny, two-person jokes.

Success story: Dinner Theater Production
Resources: Baker's Plays; Contemporary Drama Service

MEMORIAL DAY CEMETERY DECORATIONS

This is a seasonal fundraising project which will do best if it is done yearly and builds its customer base. It requires the participation of individuals skilled in preparing wreaths, flower arrangements, and stands for the decoration of cemetery sites. The arrangements may be fresh or of silk flowers and greenery.

While the wreaths can be offered ready-made prior to Memorial Day, there are many advantages to having samples and taking orders for items to be delivered at a specific location and on limited dates. At a church after services or on the property of a shopping area are two possibilities for taking orders, delivering the orders or selling ready-made wreaths and flower arrangements.

Resource: Chartwell Books

MILE OF COINS

For a simple fundraising plan, promote collecting a mile of pennies, or nickels, or dimes. Have someone good with distances and math calculate how many will be needed to make a mile (1 mile = 5,280 feet). Organize for collecting the change and keep everyone posted on your progress. If you need more than will be raised for one mile of coins, go for more miles.

MOBILE BOOTHS

Mobile booths are based on the concept of the peddler who took his wares to his customers. The merchandise can be so simple that each peddler can carry the product and just return to the supply point when he or she runs low on a particular item. Helium balloons, small food items, hats and caps, and windsocks are examples. If a partner cannot be supplied, the one person operating the mobile booth needs deep pockets or a money apron and should have at least one hand free to handle money. A better plan is to operate from a cart of some kind, a wheelbarrow, a small trailer, a luggage carrier, a suitcase on wheels, or even a child's wagon.

Salespeople for moving booths need to enjoy attracting attention. They can wear costumes or attract a crowd by doing some sort of entertainment and giving a sales spiel.

MOVIE BENEFIT

If you can find a movie theater owner or operator who is willing to help your organization, you might arrange a benefit showing of a special film. Both the film and "extras" provided by the sponsors must be able to attract patrons who will pay more than the normal movie price, or else the sponsors must get access to the special showing at a bargain cost and sell tickets to a substantial number of people.

The film might be of special interest to members of the specific local community or be related to the work of the charity sponsoring the benefit. The movie might be especially appropriate for the time period of the benefit; for example, a classic Christmas movie in December. A newly released, much advertised film should attract a crowd.

The benefit might include food, an appearance by a celebrity related to the film, presentation of door prizes, or any other attraction which would boost attendance.

MURDER MYSTERY DINNER THEATER

Offer a dinner which features an audience participation murder mystery. A group of actors and actresses assume the identities of different characters, give the audience clues by presenting scenes and answering questions, and challenge the audience members to solve a murder which is part of the plot. Part of the fun is requiring that the mystery to be solved by teams of three to five "detectives" who must agree on the answers to the questions, Who is the murderer?; What was the motive?; and What was the weapon?

A writer in your group can write the

murder mystery for you and use volunteer performers. The material must include two or more possible motives and weapons and make each character a suspect. If you do this, you need to have one or two practice performances with groups who will help you perfect your clues and the logic for your solution. Other options are to purchase a murder mystery kit or hire a cast who performs murder mysteries in other locations. Give "Outstanding Detective" certificates to those who solve the mystery correctly. The certificates and recognition may be enough for a charity event, but the group can add prizes also.

The dinner can be of any type desired. It can be at the beginning or in the middle of the murder mystery performance.

The cast of the mystery should greet the audience as they arrive and introduce themselves as the characters they play. The plot can be arranged so that some of the performers can provide music during dinner. The actors and actresses should mingle with the audience as much as possible and be available to visit and answer questions after the show.

Resources: Death in Delta; Decipher, Inc.

MUSIC FOR DONATIONS

At any crowded event in a large area, musicians can travel through the crowd, pausing frequently to perform. The hope is that the performance will attract a crowd. At times the performer can "flirt with" or "play to" a specific person. Costumes will add to the fun. The costume may consist of clothing supporting the theme of the event, the garb of a gypsy or country performer, formal wear with a top hat, or any other eye-catching apparel. Money will be earned by having a hat on the floor or ground in front of the performer; after the entertainment, the hat can be passed around the crowd by the performer, or better by a helper. An announcement and a sign on the hat should indicate that the money will be donated to the worthy cause or group.

This idea is good for singers and players of accordions, guitars, trumpets, and other portable instruments. Strolling musicians of this type are also good entertainment to be provided free by a group sponsoring a large fundraising event.

MYSTERY TRIPS

Arrange these trips just like any other except that you do not reveal the destination to the participants; allow them to guess until you arrive at each stop. The length of the trip and any special items to bring must be included in the advertising. Be sure each trip is a place the customers will enjoy. You can go for a few hours or for an extended weekend. If you have a long bus ride, provide musical entertainment or offer group participation activities as you travel.

NEEDLEWORK SHOP

Feature materials and kits for people who enjoy doing needlework projects. As much as possible, have the kits assembled by group members who are talented in needlework; this will assure that your kits are not available in stores and could provide for a greater percentage of profit. Provide samples of the finished product for each kit. Have workers prepared to demonstrate how the work is completed and to answer questions. A local store may be willing to provide some of your merchandise and give you a percentage of sales. You may also be able to secure donated materials from individuals or businesses.

Resources: American School of Needlework; Annie's Attic, Inc.; Chilton Book Company; Crafts 'N Things; Dover Publications, Inc.; Mallard Press; McCall Pattern Co.; Sterling Publishing Co., Inc.; The DMC Corporation; Workbasket Magazine

PANCAKE BREAKFAST

Plan a pancake breakfast for a Saturday or Sunday morning. In addition to several types of pancakes and toppings, offer sausage, bacon, ham and drinks. Pancakes with chocolate chip or raisin faces are fun if children are present. Fruit salad would offer a lighter choice.

Unless the cooks for the pancakes are very experienced, they need some practice sessions with their batter on the grill they will be using for the breakfast.

PANCAKE DAY

Start with a pancake breakfast featuring a pancake-eating contest. In addition to rewarding the eating contest winner, sell chances which have a time written on them; the purchaser with the time closest to when the last bite of pancake is eaten for the contest wins a prize.

After breakfast have separate races for men and women during which the contestants must race while they flip a pancake in a frying pan. Prizes go to those who have flipped the pancake at least five times without dropping it and cross the finish line first. Have a race between the winners of the men's and women's races using fresh pancakes. The winner is rewarded with a prize and honors such as a crown and a sash naming him or her Pancake King or Queen.

PARADE

Sometimes organizing a parade is close to being in the category of a community service rather than a fundraiser. However, profit can be made from charging a fee for entries in the floats, marching groups, classic cars, and many other categories and awarding prizes to the winners as determined by judges. A beauty contest to select the queen of the parade can be sponsored by the group. People who gather to watch the parade are potential customers for food and merchandise. The committee must have the support and assistance of the local officials in regard to permits, route preparation, and crowd control. Businesses in the area should be supportive and willing to donate services or money to support the project.

Resources: STUMPS—One Party Place

PARENTS' NIGHT OUT

Plan a children's party which provides activities for children of all ages which are led and supervised by volunteers who wish to help raise money for the cause. Advertise it as a Parents' Night Out. Friday and Saturday nights would probably be favorite nights for this activity. A regular time, such as the first Saturday of each month, might help build the crowd and save on advertising. If offered in the weeks before Christmas, Parents' Night Out can be advertised as a shopping opportunity for the parents.

Resources: McFarland & Company, Inc., Publishers; Pack-O-Fun; Plays, Inc., Publishers; Sterling Publishing Co., Inc.; The H.W. Wilson Company

PERSONALIZED ITEMS BOOTH

If you have group members talented at personalizing items under pressure, they can probably do a good business with a few well chosen products.

Have samples with names already on the item and then have the item in several colors or styles.

Children's items are especially popular with names added. Banks, cups, bibs, headbands, signs for room doors, towels, lunch boxes and pencil boxes are examples of merchandise which can be ready to have names added. Names added to pet dishes, bandannas, toys, Christmas stockings, and towels appeal to pet owners. Other items ready to be personalized could include shirts, tote bags, nylon wallets, umbrellas, body size towels, neckties, bowling or golfer towels, rock paperweights, picture frames—in fact, any craft item or other product that can be personalized. If you are selling in the fall, attractive tree ornaments and Christmas stockings are an excellent choice for personalizing.

PET BOOTH

Feature everything related to family pets. Dog and cat items will be most popular but you can include articles for birds, fish, turtles and other less common pets. Items for sale can include collars of all sizes, toys for the animals, beds and resting pillows and pads, scratching pads for cats, towels with an appropriate appliqué or lettering, food bowls, snacks, Christmas stockings or ornaments, ribbon bows, jackets, dog bandannas, fish bowls and decorations, bird cages, pet carriers, brushes for the pet and to remove pet hair, cloth cat sacks with crinkling filling, and catnip-filled cloth mice, balls or pillows. Volunteers can make some of the items; others must be solicited for contribution or purchased at a price low enough to allow for markup. Try for return agreements on purchased items which do not sell.

Related fundraising idea: Animal World Booth
Resources: Cat Fancy; Dog Fancy

PET SHOW

In order to do this well, someone in the group needs to be familiar with how legitimate dog and cat shows work. Then a committee can adapt some of the procedures and rules to feature categories such as pets in costume, pets under 3 months of age, pedigree unknown, and most unusual pet. Charge entrance fees, admittance, and give prizes to the pets and perhaps door prizes to the audience.

PET SITTING

There is significant earning potential in caring for pets while their owners are on vacations or business trips. The service can be based on visiting the owner's home, taking the pet to the home of a volunteer worker or caring for the animal in facilities the group provides and maintains.

PET WALKING

For many owners, pets are special and pampered. Busy owners and those unable to exercise their pets might pay volunteers from your organization to walk their dog on a regular schedule. Joggers might offer a jogging service to appropriate animals. With the proceeds going to a worthy cause, this should be an attractive service for sale.

PETTING PLACE

Locate groups or businesses that will help you arrange a place for children to pet animals. A pet shop, animal shelter, or zoo might cooperate for the publicity and goodwill. Offer food for the children to feed the animals, if appropriate. Adults must be in complete control of the area and the animals with parents encouraged or required to participate in supervision.

PHOTOGRAPH PROPS

Provide interesting settings for pictures. Charge a modest fee for people with a camera to use your props and more for a worker to take a picture with an instant camera. If you have someone who can make props, you can save them and use them over and over. Examples are old fashioned "stocks" for confining arms, legs, heads or some combination or a jail window. Another approach is figures painted on boards with an opening for the head. Children would like their faces on a cowboy, a princess, a pirate, Donald Duck, E.T., an Indian, a witch, a lion, etc. Adults might like a pioneer, a saloon girl, a pregnant lady, a curvy body in a bikini, a belly dancer; an astronaut; a muscular male figure; an injured person with casts, bandages and crutches, etc.

Some customers might pay to have a picture of them "driving" some interesting vehicle, like a motorcycle, racing car, fire engine, police car, classic car, or pink convertible. A cooperative horse, pony, camel, parrot, or snake could contribute by being a prop for a picture.

Provide a variety of costumes in various sizes—old time clothes, western or saloon girl outfits, outrageous hats, etc. A costume rental business or a theatrical group might loan you outfits for the booth. If the booth will be an annual event, a talented seamstress could make a few pieces of clothing each year to add to the group's inventory.

The props could be suggested by the theme of your event.

PHOTOGRAPHER—MOVING

A photographer in costume, with an instant camera and a lot of film, can take and sell informal pictures at many events. Pictures of children and teens and closeup portrait pictures are good prospects. If there are workers in costume at an event, try pictures of them interacting with others. Charge enough to make up for the pictures which will not sell.

PHOTOGRAPHS BOOTH

Picture taking can be a fundraiser which requires only a modest amount of capital and volunteer time. The necessities are a camera, a photographer, a money-record keeper and at least one special feature. Children of all ages like to have their picture taken with Santa, the Easter Bunny, or a clown. Sometimes a background will sell pictures. A decorated arch or a large heart in February are examples of traditional backdrops. Consider the location of the booth, the time of year and the theme of the event. If you have more than one good idea and can arrange to offer a choice, do so.

Polaroid pictures finish the sale on the spot, and when there is more than one person in the picture, you often are asked to take more than one picture of the same group. If you are using a regular camera, collect your fee, give a receipt and designate a time and place for the picture to be picked up. Offer a mailing service for those who want it. With your picture, send a price list for additional prints. With two cameras you can offer either instant or standard pictures with a minimum of extra effort.

Resource: STUMPS—One Party Place

PICTURES WITH IMPERSONATORS

Do you have workers who can be made to look like famous people? If so, offer polaroid pictures with impersonators. You could have an Elvis, Marilyn Monroe, Madonna, Michael Jackson, or any celebrity who has a distinctive look. For ideas note whom entertainers impersonate. If customers have their own cameras, charge a reduced fee for the impersonator to pose with them.

PIE SUPPER

This old fashioned way of raising money calls for group members to bring homemade pies in decorated boxes. An auctioneer auctions the boxes to the highest bidder. The buyers have the opportunity to share the pie and conversation with the person who brought the pie. A similar event would feature picnic basket dinners.

This event can work in any group which has a number of people willing to participate. The highest prices will come from competition—serious or in fun—for the pies or meals which have a special appeal for the bidders.

PIZZAS

Pizzas are a very popular food. A group can take orders for pizza to be delivered hot at a designated time and place. The pizza can be made by members of the group or bought at a discount from a pizzeria. Some companies promote frozen pizza sales for group fundraising projects. Of course, pizza can be the main feature of a lunch or dinner or be sold at a booth, if baking facilities are available.

PLANT AND FLOWER BOOTH

Enlist a person who loves plants and flowers to organize for a plant and flower booth. A local florist or greenhouse may be willing to stock this booth

and give the organization a percentage of the sales. The other option is to have plants grown especially for the project.

The following items can be sold in addition to plants and flowers of all kinds: bulbs; seedlings; seeds; shrubs; gardening tools; books about plants, flowers, flower arranging; pots and containers appropriate for plants and flower arrangements; wind chimes; sundials; bird baths; and anything else that would be found in a garden or yard area.

As much as possible, try to keep in the booth a volunteer who can answer questions about the nature and care of the plants and flowers.

The sale of plants and flowers might be a fundraising project independent of a bazaar or event where they are in a booth. Think creatively and perhaps the organization can set up a stand that will operate during the period of heavy plant and flower sales.

Resource: Smithmark Publishers, Inc.

PLANT SITTING

The customer should supply written instructions for the care desired for each plant. The service should be more expensive if it requires house calls than if the plants are cared for in the home of the care giver. Consider the time and trouble of the worker when setting your price. If the group has access to an appropriate location, you might want to offer pickup, care in a central location, and delivery back home of the treasured plants.

PLAYS AND MUSICALS

Inviting the public to a play or musical is a popular fundraising activity. The first requirement for this project is a strong director who can enlist and or lead the performers. The facility will limit the technical aspects of the performance and the number of tickets which can be sold. This project usually involves expenses which must be met whether or not the tickets sell well. Be sure to take into account the royalty payments required. It is usually good to have more than one performance in order to attract more paying customers and multiply the use of the scenery, props and costumes.

If your group does not feel qualified to produce a play or musical, perhaps you can become partners with a community or school theatrical group or choir. Your group can handle all aspects of the project except the actual performance for a percentage of the profit or ticket sales.

Success story: Dinner Theater Production
Resources: Baker's Plays; Contemporary Drama Service; Eldridge Publishing Company; Plays, Inc., Publishers

POEMS FOR THE OCCASION

The services of an amateur poet can allow you to sell personalized poems for special occasions. The sales force can obtain information to be used by the poet in composing the poem. Someone with access to appropriate computer software can produce the poem text complete with appropriate illustrations and print the poem on quality paper. Remember the considerable personalized service and the uniqueness of the product when setting your price. If the team of poets can produce under pressure, this service and the product could be offered in a booth at a bazaar.

PONY RIDES

If you have access to a gentle, dependable pony or horse, offer rides with plenty of parent supervision. Don't forget preparations for keeping your riding area as clean as possible if you are not in a pasture area.

POPCORN

Some malls have shops devoted entirely to the sale of popcorn in many flavors and in many types of containers. A group can sell packaged popcorn, popcorn from a popping machine, or a variety of flavors of popcorn from a more elaborate operation. This is a good item for both a booth and roving vendors at a large event. Popcorn can be purchased in bulk or popped and flavored by the

workers. Keep in mind that the odor of popcorn is wonderful advertising and attracts customers.

Resource: Noble Popcorn

PORTRAIT CENTER

Provide space for a professional photographer to set up at one of your fundraising events and sell packaged professional pictures. Your agreement will provide for your organization to receive a percentage of sales or a set amount on each package sold. A volunteer will probably be expected to deliver the pictures for the photographer.

PROFESSIONAL ENTERTAINMENT

Sponsor a program by professional entertainers who will appeal to the members of your community. The entertainment can range from a musical group to puppets to a dramatic performance. You provide the place, advertisements that feature your good cause, the sales force for tickets, and related events. Your ticket price might include a social hour before or after the entertainment and refreshments or the opportunity to purchase refreshments. Be sure to have an agreement with the entertainers which clearly specifies all aspects of the financial agreement.

PROGRESSIVE DINNER

A meal is planned which has a variety of courses served one course per location with the guests moving from place to place. The locations may be in several homes within walking distance of each other, or vans or limousines might be provided for moving from place to place. The main course could be in a restaurant or dining hall; appetizers would be pleasant in a formal garden or a room in a historical house; entertainment may be featured with dessert. During bad weather a progressive dinner could move from room to room in the same building (perhaps a church or school) with each room decorated in a distinctive manner. The arrangements and food for a progressive dinner can range from the simple to the elaborate and be priced accordingly. This idea works for teenagers and adults of all ages.

PUMPKINS PAINTED

In October persons talented at painting faces on pumpkins can offer them for sale wherever they can arrange a booth. If an artist is painting a face on a pumpkin and several finished ones are on display, the process and product are bound to attract attention and the pumpkins should sell well. Having a display of pictures of various painted pumpkins will allow the taking of special orders.

RAFFLES

For a raffle to be a successful fundraiser, it is imperative that your group select a prize which appeals to your potential customers. Businesses sometimes will donate an appropriate prize or give your group a good price on an item you want for a prize.

Cash is a favorite prize. The amount can be a set amount or the amount or number of prizes can be set by the sales. Some organizations offer a fifty-fifty split; half of the sales money to the organization and half as prizes. Other prizes to consider are quilts; afghans; handmade tables, bookcases, doll houses, and other wood products; silver tea sets; bicycles; VCRs; televisions; sports equipment; food baskets; catered dinners for 10 or 20; season tickets to a theater or sports events; a car; a boat; a cruise for two. The prize possibilities are endless; the important thing is to match the prize to the customers.

As important as the prize is to a raffle, the sales force is equally important. Those who sell tickets must be hardworking and dedicated. You might offer prizes for those who sell the most tickets. Consider enlisting a group of teenagers and training them to sell. Involve as many sellers as you can and meet to plan a sales campaign. Sell raffle tickets wherever you can find a crowd. Make a ceremony of drawing the ticket and do it in front of as large a crowd as possible.

Resources: Ace-Acme; St. Louis Carnival Supply

RECORDED GREETINGS

Offer customers an appointment to record a tape for the VCR or a tape recorder. The recording session can produce greetings for Christmas, Mother's

Day, Father's Day, an anniversary, graduation, retirement, birthday, or any other special occasion or just a "thinking of you" message. This can be greetings from one person or a group. Members of the committee probably can obtain the use of the needed equipment and set it up in a location with good acoustics and no outside noise. Create a number of scripts for the customers who want suggestions for content. Have appropriate poems, greeting card messages and songs available to provide inspiration for greetings. Offer for sale containers suitable for mailing both video and audio tapes.

RECORDED INTERVIEWS

Many people would like to have a tape for their VCR or tape recorder of some relative or friend telling about family history, the "good ole days," their favorite jokes, etc. A team of volunteers—one to operate the equipment and one to conduct the interview—could earn money creating the tape for the customer. Extra copies of the tape would also be available for purchase. The price of the service could be determined by the length of the tape. Prepare a list of interview questions and allow the customer to check the ones which should be used. There should be an understanding that the person conducting the interview could pursue interesting topics. The person doing the interview needs a pleasant voice and a warm, interested manner. The recordings could be done in a studio-type setting or in the home of the person being interviewed.

Resources: Banner Blue Software; McFarland & Company, Inc., Publishers

RED, WHITE AND BLUE BOOTH

This idea works best around the Fourth of July. The merchandise can be anything in red, white or bright blue or any combination of the colors. Patriotic items such as flags, prints of famous documents, and political cartoons are also good stock. A variation of this idea can apply to a booth featuring the colors of the local high school. In this case the merchandise would be in the school colors and feature items with the school's name or mascot on them.

Resource: Dover Publications, Inc.

ROAST AND TOAST

Your group might host a banquet featuring a "Roast and Toast" of a prominent local celebrity or leader. If you don't have a celebrity type available, consider the high school coach or principal or the 20-year senior sponsor. A church might roast and toast the pastor or other well-liked member. Most organizations have a leader or a practical joker to feature. The guest of honor needs to have a sense of humor and be willing—behind the scenes— to steer the committees to participants who have good stories to share about embarrassing events, etc. Publicize the recipient of the profits and keep the charge high enough to have a worthy contribution for your good cause.

RUMMAGE SALES

If you have a place to store the donated junk and treasures people are willing to donate, consider periodic rummage sales to benefit your cause. Rummage sales, garage sales, and flea markets have much in common since they sell secondhand items. More creative names are often used for this type of event. Attic Treasures, White Elephants, This and That for Sale, Collector's Corner, and Thieves' Market are examples of titles that have been used.

Keep the displays as uncluttered as possible. Group things of a similar type together and then provide an Odds and Ends section for the more unique. All items should be clean, and clothing sells better if it is ironed. Be sure prices are firmly attached but in a way which allows them to be removed without damaging the item. Have boxes, sacks, newspapers, and string available for packaging merchandise sold. Adequate change makes the event smoother and probably increases sales.

Enlist adequate salespeople. Have someone in each area responsible for the money and have the cash box always supervised. Don't forget a committee to store unsold items for the next sale or to arrange for a charity such as the Salvation Army or Goodwill to pick up the items that are left at the end of the sale.

Related fundraising ideas: Garage Sales; Thrift Shops; Flea Markets

SALAD LUNCHEON

A salad luncheon will generally appeal more to women than the men. Advertise it in the businesses close to where the luncheon will be held and serve between 11 A.M. and 2 P.M. If members of the group donate a variety of salads and desserts, the income will be much greater and the work of the committee easier. Volunteers will prepare rolls, butter, crackers, and drinks and set up the items needed for serving. Prior reservations are needed and perhaps the tickets should be sold ahead of time. One price and a buffet setup are the easiest way to deal with variety created by donations of food.

SAND ART BOOTH

Color sand a variety of basic and complementary colors by mixing white sand and powdered tempera paint. If you must use liquid tempera paint, spread the colored sand to dry several days before using. Provide a container for each color of sand, several scoops, funnels, and clear glass and plastic containers. Set a price for each container according to its quality and size and allow customers to use the colors of sand they wish to create sand art in their container. The containers can range from clear empty catsup bottles to glass vases to fish bowls. Containers can be purchased wholesale or at discount stores, but you should obtain as many as possible as donations. Have some attractive examples of what can be created; sell them if someone shows interest and create new examples.

SANDWICH SHOPPE

A sandwich shoppe, booth, or bar offers a variety of sandwiches and beverages. Offer a variety of breads and fillings and wrap the sandwiches in clear wrap. Give access to items which can be added to the sandwiches or have workers who are obviously practicing sanitary procedures assemble the sandwiches or add dressings, pickles, lettuce, and other toppings upon order. Do not offer sandwiches if you do not have the facilities to keep the food free from contamination.

SAYINGS AND QUOTES BOOTH

Sell items such as signs, plaques, posters, shirts, mugs, caps, and paperweights which feature sayings or quotes. Illustrate the items with appropriate pictures when possible. The following are some of the sayings and quotes which can be found on signs and merchandise:

TEACHERS HAVE CLASS

THREE REASONS TO BE A TEACHER: JUNE,
    JULY, AUGUST

FLYING IS HIGH ADVENTURE

I'M A HAIRSTYLIST—I COULD TELL YOU
    STORIES THAT WOULD CURL YOUR
    HAIR

CARPENTERS ARE A CUT ABOVE THE REST

NURSES CAN REALLY TAKE THE PRESSURE

NURSING IS MY BAG

BOSS OF FLOSS

HUG A FIRE FIGHTER—FEEL WARM ALL OVER

PLUMBERS LIKE IT PIPING HOT

FORGET THE DOG—BEWARE OF THE KIDS

YOUR DOG LOVES YOU WHEN NOBODY ELSE DOES

PROTECTED BY AN ATTACK CAT

MY DOG WALKS ALL OVER ME (with pawprints)

RING THE BELL FOR MAID SERVICE—IF NO ANSWER, DO IT YOURSELF

KITCHEN CLOSED—THIS CHICK HAS HAD IT (picture of chicken)

I CAME, I SAW, I CHARGED IT

UDDER CHAOS LIVES HERE (on a cow)

IF MAMA AIN'T HAPPY, NOBODY IS HAPPY

IF PAPA AIN'T HAPPY, NOBODY CARES

BORN TO SHOP

LIFE IS UNCERTAIN, EAT DESSERT FIRST

WHO NEEDS SANTA? I'VE GOT GRANDMA

ONE NICE PERSON AND ONE OLD GROUCH LIVE HERE

WORLD'S LARGEST SOURCE OF NATURAL GAS

RETIRED AND DRIVING MY WIFE CRAZY

LAUGHTER IS THE BEST MEDICINE

I'M SOMEONE'S FAVORITE BALD GUY

BALD MEN ARE SEXIER!

ONCE I WAS A MILLIONAIRE
    THEN MY MOM THREW MY BASEBALL CARDS AWAY

PRIVATE WORKSHOP—LEAVE MY MESS ALONE

I LOVE TO WATCH THE SEASONS CHANGE
    BASEBALL, FOOTBALL, BASKETBALL, HOCKEY

I LIKE WHEN THE SEASONS CHANGE / FISHING TO HUNTING

IF IT GOES RIGHT, IT'S A SLICE
    IF IT GOES LEFT, IT'S A HOOK
    IF IT GOES STRAIGHT, IT'S A MIRACLE (golf symbol)

HUNTERS WILL DO ANYTHING FOR A BUCK
HUNTERS OUT FOR A BUCK
BOWLER OF THE YEAR
GOLFER OF THE YEAR
FIRST CLASS GOLFER
FIRST CLASS FISHERMAN
A BAD DAY AT THE BRIDGE TABLE IS STILL BETTER THAN CLEANING
    HOUSE
FISHING IS NOT A MATTER OF LIFE OR DEATH—IT IS MUCH MORE
    IMPORTANT
OLD FISHERMEN NEVER DIE—THEY JUST SMELL THAT WAY
I'M 16! GIVE ME YOUR KEYS, GIVE ME THE CREDIT CARDS AND GET OUT
    OF MY WAY
I'M 17 / WARNING / TEENAGER ON THE LOOSE
I'M NOT 40 / I'M 18 WITH 22 YEARS OF EXPERIENCE
I'M NOT 50 / I'M 18 WITH 32 YEARS OF EXPERIENCE
BIG SISTER / LITTLE BROTHER
BIG BROTHER / LITTLE SISTER
NO SWEAT! MY FAITH KEEPS ME COOL
FAITH MAKES THE IMPOSSIBLE POSSIBLE
GREAT SPIRIT HELP ME NEVER TO JUDGE ANOTHER UNTIL I HAVE WALKED
    IN HIS MOCCASINS
I'M NOT OPINIONATED—I'M JUST ALWAYS RIGHT

The possibilities for sayings and quotes are many. Choose those appropriate for your potential customers and the event at which you will have your booth.

Offering to fill special orders will improve sales. Often the customer wants a combination of saying and merchandise different from what you have in your booth. Be sure to plan your policy before the event. Know how much deposit you require, how long it will be before the special order is ready, how the merchandise will be delivered, and what your refund policy will be. If you plan to take orders, have an order form ready.

SELLING PRODUCTS

The selling of products is a common way for groups to raise money. Selecting a good product can be tricky, but with care almost any size group can raise money through sales. Look for a product that will appeal to the general public, not just a select group. Limit the money you pay for inventory as much as possible; negotiate for the right to return merchandise or materials you do not use. If you agree to sell a company's product for them, ask them for references from other fundraisers who have worked with them. Try for a profit of 50 percent or more of the retail price on each item and think carefully before you settle for less than 30 percent. Read your sales agreement carefully and discuss any section you are unsure about.

Products can be sold at special events, before and after meetings, and by salespeople to family, friends, and coworkers on an individual basis. Accurate and up-to-date records of inventory, expenses, sales and profits are important.

Success stories: Avon Fundraiser; Candy Sale

SELLING SERVICES

Sell the work of your volunteers instead of selling things. Promote a specific service for a limited period of time or provide an ongoing service. It may be best to begin a service by advertising it for a limited period of time and see if you have the workers with the time and desire to undertake it for a longer period.

For ideas, check the Yellow Pages to see what services are offered commercially and discuss in your group what services they would like to purchase. Businesses might use your group as a temporary work force for jobs such as inventory or mailings and, in return, give a donation to your good cause.

SERENADES FOR ALL OCCASIONS

If your volunteers include soloists or small singing groups who are willing, offer serenades for all occasions. Your vocalists can sing without accompaniment or play a tape with the music recorded. Develop a list of songs which may be chosen in honor of birthdays, Valentine's Day, a proposal of marriage, Secretary's Day, promotions, retirements and other special days. Some songs could be appropriate for a message of "I love you," "Thank you," or even "I'm sorry." Before starting an ongoing fundraiser in the form of serenades, let your workers try the project for a Secretary's Day or Valentine's Day. After the serenade, the person accompanying the singer or singers may present one artificial flower attached to a card which indicates who arranged for the serenade.

A related offering could be a singing message delivered by telephone.

This could be less time consuming for the volunteer workers and much less expensive for the customer.

Success story: Valentine Balloons and Serenades
Resources: Lonestar Technologies, Ltd.; Music Dispatch

SHIRTS BOOTH

One shirt booth cannot offer merchandise with the full variety possible in this category. It is best to limit the shirts available to a few styles in all sizes and a variety of colors.

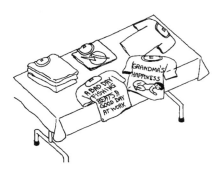

Consider taking a survey of members of the organization and community to see what type of decorated shirts they own or have seen that they would recommend be sold. Don't forget to ask some children and teenagers what type of shirts they like. If this idea isn't practical, form a committee to make the decision on what to stock on the theory that several can decide better than one or two and a plan is better than no plan.

After the shirts are collected for sale, take pictures of those you can offer for special order. Create order forms and decide your policy for when the shirts will be ready and how they will reach the customer. Will you require a down payment or complete prepayment? Do you guarantee satisfaction? How long before the shirt will be ready? You may decide that you do not want to take orders, but you need to make your decisions before the sale. If your shirts are popular, someone will certainly want one that is a different style, size, or color from what you have.

If volunteers donate decorated shirts and will take back those not sold, you are on safe financial ground. If the committee must provide the shirts and other materials used, think long and hard about your pricing and potential profit and what you will do with shirts not sold.

T-shirts and sweatshirts are the most commonly used for decorating. Western and southwestern shirts are also an option. Some with experience in this area say that females prefer loose and large in sizing and males prefer a tighter fit. While this is a generalization, it seems worth considering.

Shirts can be decorated in many ways, such as: painting, patchwork, appliquéd shapes, iron-on and enhanced designs, fringe, lace, buttons, ribbons, colorful glue-on stones, sequin cloth or strips, braid, etc. Only the informed will appreciate the time spent on a shirt. Try for an expensive look that can be achieved with a minimum of time.

SHOPPING SERVICE FOR SHUT-INS

Charge a modest yearly membership fee which entitles customers to hire volunteers to shop for them at a specified hourly rate. Coordinator volunteers accept the requests and enlist a volunteer shopper who is available at a time acceptable to the customer. The charge for the shopping service goes to the worthy cause. In some circumstances accepting donations rather than a set hourly fee might work to everyone's advantage. Some customers will have limited funds and others can be more generous. Some shoppers will complete their assignment at a faster rate than others. A few customers may take advantage of the workers with a donation system, but this policy can be changed after a period of time, if needed.

SHOWS FOR KIDS

Organize Saturday or Sunday afternoon entertainments for children. Gear the show to attract a specific age group since that will influence the type of show offered. The entertainment could be a puppet show, a talent show, cartoons or children's movies, a magic show, children singing and dancing, clown acts, teenagers acting out nursery rhymes or fairy tales, or adult actors and actresses portraying classic children tales like "Red Riding Hood." Check with local drama groups in the community—perhaps at school or a church. If your group includes a person who likes to direct drama projects, perhaps he or she will enlist volunteers to perform a series of shows. Allow parents to buy tickets and attend but also offer supervision so parents can drop their children off and pick them up later.

Resources: Contemporary Drama Service; Dover Publications, Inc.; Eldridge Publishing Company; Meriwether Publishing Ltd., Publisher; Piccadilly Books; Plays, Inc., Publishers; The H.W. Wilson Company

SHUT-INS TELEPHONE CHECK

This fundraising project is especially good if you have dependable volunteers who spend most of their time at home and like to talk on the telephone. For a fee, call shut-ins or those without family members in town during a set time period each day. The persons receiving the calls would agree to notify the caller if they will not be home during that period of time. The callers will chat a few minutes if they receive an answer but will have emergency phone numbers to call if they need to notify a neighbor or relative to check on the person who does not answer. This task might be daily for some volunteers, but it will probably prevent burnout to put the workers on duty one week every month or two. Sell the service for three months to a year. Advertise the service as a potential Christmas, birthday, Mother's Day, or Father's Day gift. Be sure there is an agreement which clearly defines the service and its policies.

SKATING PARTY

The operators of a roller skating or ice skating rink can be approached for a group price or a private time which will allow the group to make a profit in return for its promotion efforts. First ask for the rink to donate skating time as a public service for your cause. If the management gives the group free time or a significant price break, advertise the rink's sponsorship in all flyers, posters, and press releases for the party.

SOUTH OF THE BORDER THEME

This theme brings to mind food, clothing, music, merchandise and decorations associated with Mexico. It could be expanded to include the things associated with countries in South America. With the right cook in charge, more authentic food can be added to the popular tacos, enchiladas, taco salads, etc. Workers have opportunities to be in costume with colorful cotton clothings, easily obtained hats, and easy-to-make serapes. Some may have access to attractive formal wear with Spanish influences. Music and dance performances and taped music will add to the atmosphere. Don't forget large paper flower groupings, cactus and other plants in ceramic pots, Mexican hats, and travel posters for decorations. Having volunteers of Mexican heritage will take care of most of the problems that may arise with this theme.

Resources: Barnes & Noble; Dover Publications, Inc.; Plays, Inc., Publishers; St. Louis Carnival Supply

SPAGHETTI SUPPER

Spaghetti suppers are often popular, especially if a talented and enthusiastic cook is in charge. Salad, with a choice of dressing, hot garlic bread and desserts seem to be the basic expected items. Other foods can be added to fit the situation, customers and workers.

SPRING HOUSE CLEANING SERVICE

Organize workers into house cleaning crews and offer to do spring house cleaning. Have a checklist of tasks you will do and offer customers a price based on the tasks and the size of the home.

Both working women and older homeowners will be prime candidates for your advertising.

Resource: Writer's Digest Books

SPRING THEME

Most people get spring fever in some form each year. Your group can use spring as a theme for an event and utilize that seasonal interest in planting flowers and gardens and participating in other warm weather activities. Spring also heightens interest in vacations for many. Easter is a major holiday which offers symbols and music related to spring. Pastel colors are commonly associated with the season.

Sales opportunities exist for kites, windsocks, birds, bird houses, and bird baths. Families enjoy opportunities to feed fish, ducks, and goats, and petting zoos and pony rides are popular. You might also sell chances on a lawn mower, a two-for-the-price-of-one cruise or resort week, or season passes to the local pool or amusement park.

STRAWBERRY FEAST

Strawberry season offers the opportunity to feature strawberry desserts such as shortcake, sundaes, homemade ice cream, and fresh strawberries with homemade cookies. The strawberry feast can be part of a dance or music performance, or an event following a meeting or church service. This idea will also work as a booth at a bazaar or festival, especially if the group can provide tables and chairs in the shade or a quiet corner in a building.

Success story: Strawberry Festival

T-SHIRTS DECORATED

Allow individuals to decorate their own T-shirts using the paints and other materials made available by the group. Have glue, needles and thread, and an iron and ironing board available, as well as a wide variety of materials and sample decorated shirts. Seek to have most of the materials donated so that the fee charged for the work session will be primarily profit. Workers should be available to encourage customers and help them with the shirts. The workshop should be a recreational experience as well as making the decorating experience easier for the participants. The admission fee might include simple refreshments.

The time of year might make it more appropriate to decorate sweatshirts, or to give the participants a choice of T-shirts or sweatshirts.

TALENT CONTEST

Have a competition in one or more categories of performance. Charge an entry fee to be paid by the performer or sponsor. Offer prizes appropriate for your situation. Judges should be respected individuals and their method of voting as objective as possible. Consider allowing the audience to vote for their favorite performer in some categories. Charge admission and sell food. Other fundraisers, such as raffles, cookbooks, and bake sales, might be held with the event. Contests in individual song, dance, and dramatic reading would be appropriate with a choir, band, or cheerleading competition.

TALENT SHOW

Enlist entertainers for a talent show; ask for an audition to be sure of the kind of performance planned. Seek a variety of types or performers—musical, dance, drama, serious, funny. If your group does not include an abundance of talent ready to perform, use contacts in theater groups, schools and churches to refer you to amateur performers. Teachers of dance, voice, and instruments will probably help you contact their most talented students. Don't forget short skits, comedy routines, and dramatic speeches as potential acts.

Resources: Contemporary Drama Service; Eldridge Publishing Company; Music Dispatch

TASTING PARTIES

A tasting party is an event at which the guests are provided with a variety of food in small portions with the expectation that they will try the different items. The tasting party can feature any single type of food or every kind. The guests might sample a variety of cheeses and crackers; a selection of cubed ham, lunch meats, and sausage; various fondue combinations; small portions of gourmet desserts; samples of casserole dishes; vegetables of several kinds fried in breading or batter; pizza with different toppings; bread of many types; fruit slices with complementary dips, etc. The food can be prepared by the members of the group having the fundraiser or maybe donated by companies. Recipes and order blanks need to be provided if appropriate. A group selling a cookbook might launch sales with a tasting party.

TEA ROOM EVENT

Sell tickets and host a group for an old fashioned ladies' tea room event. Have tables with cloth coverings, napkins, napkin rings, silver, centerpieces, delicate dishes, silver tea services and waitresses in black dresses and white aprons and little hats. Have soft music playing and serve the food in a slow, relaxed manner. The menu could be salads, small sandwiches, relish dish items, fruit, and small elegant desserts. If you want to have entertainment, consider a fashion show of old fashioned dresses, a small group of live musicians playing classical music or a soloist singing vintage songs.

This would be a good mother and daughter event, perhaps for Mother's Day.

THEATER PARTY

Make arrangements with a theater for a group rate on tickets which you resell as part of a package which includes some type of event before or after the show. A dinner or reception with a star, members of the cast, or the director would be a natural attraction. If that is not an option, a tour backstage and on stage before or after the performance might be possible. If the individuals directly involved with the production are not available, ask the publicity director to arrange a brief presentation about the play or production by a knowledgeable speaker.

THRIFT SHOP

Thrift shops often start after a group has had success with periodic rummage sales and decides to turn the sale of donated secondhand items into a business. The thrift shop is in a permanent location and open regular hours, even though the regular hours may be as little as one afternoon a week. The merchandise is constantly changing as items are sold and new items are donated. Children's clothing, women's clothing, small appliances in good condition, jewelry, decorative items and dishes reportedly sell well at most thrift shops.

Some thrift shops offer the donor a percentage of the selling price. This seems to increase the quantity and quality of items donated. A thrift shop can begin small and in a location with free rent and then grow and move when sales improve.

Related fundraising ideas: Rummage Sales; Garage Sales; Flea Markets

TOURNAMENT

Think creatively about holding a tournament. Traditional sporting events are definite possibilities. You may be able to have company or group basketball, softball, golf, bowling, tennis, or other sports teams compete against each other in a tournament for a trophy or prizes. Tournaments could also be held for chess, checkers, Scrabble, bridge and other card games, horseshoes, badminton, table tennis, miniature golf, computer hangman, pinball, etc.

The group's money can come from the sale of tickets for observers, entry fees, food sales, ads in a program book, and products such as special T-shirts and hats.

The tournament may need different categories of contestants divided by age or sex. Enlist celebrities—national or local—to compete or judge, if possible. A tournament requires detailed organization and a substantial number of volunteers to work. The ideal is to have a great many members of the community involved.

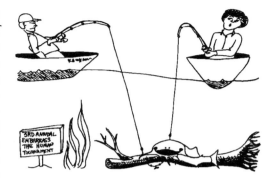

Related fundraising idea: Golf Scramble

TOURS

People enjoy having a tour leader organize a trip for them. They are especially willing to pay for the service when the money is going for a worthy cause. The organizers plan the itinerary, provide transportation, make reservations, plan for meals and go along to provide information and solve problems.

Wherever you live you can find potential tour sites. You can take groups to sporting events, programs of various types, parks and other places with nature attractions, farms, factories, shopping outlet malls, flea markets, garage sales, museums, festivals, carnivals, and bazaars. The tour can be through the historical section of a town, city or countryside. A trip can take a few hours or several days.

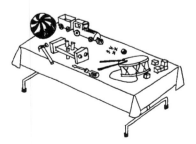

TOYS BOOTH

A booth with a wide variety of toys will be an attraction for all children at an event, plus their parents and grandparents. Offer handmade items such as dolls, doll clothes, stuffed animals, and wooden puzzles. Sell toys on consignment from a wholesaler or cooperative retailer. Have a section for recycled toys which have been donated and repaired as needed. Sporting goods and games are appropriate for this booth also. Teenagers make good salespersons for this booth, especially in dealing with younger children.

Resources: Ace-Acme; Dover Publications, Inc.

TREASURE HUNT

A treasure hunt can be geared to children, adults, family groups, or any other category of individuals or teams you think will pay money to participate. The hunt can be outside in a park area, in a large school or government building, or perhaps in a shopping mall where the business people are willing to be part of the hunt. The prize can be for the first person or group to arrive at the destination or there can be an achievement prize for all who finish at the ending point by an established deadline. Each location on the hunt can contain the next clue or a small item to be collected to prove that the person or group has been to that landmark. Refreshments or a meal should end the hunt so the participants can enjoy visiting and sharing their adventures.

In structuring a treasure hunt, start by planning your beginning point and the ending destination; the clues and intermediate points can then be developed by one or two creative people. Be sure to keep all but the beginning point top secret until the hunt.

Another type of hunt is an "information hunt" which requires teams to determine the answers to a set of questions related to a specific location or area, such as a museum or some type of fairly large educational display. The prizes can be awarded to the first group to deliver all, or the most, correct answers to the judge by a specified time.

TRIVIA NIGHT

Trivia night calls for a large hall, tables and chairs for the groups, a public address system, and someone to organize and direct the trivia competition. The basic idea is for the participants to be in groups which work together to answer trivia questions. In agreement with the guidelines announced, the groups receive points toward prizes or chances on prizes awarded at the end of the evening. Prizes may be awarded for each set of questions. Some of the competitions may be by a person representing each group; the first group representative who writes down the correct answer and delivers it to the appointed person is declared the winner.

Snacks—popcorn, pretzels, desserts, etc.—and coffee and other drinks can be part of the ticket price. Some of the food items may be donated to increase the profit from the project.

It is wise to eliminate trivia games as sources of questions. A library or bookstore will provide books with appropriate questions, if the person in charge needs a resource.

VALENTINE BALLOONS

Take orders for helium-filled balloons to be delivered on Valentine's Day. Have the customer fill out an order form and complete a message form to be attached to the ribbons tied to the balloon(s).

Have the advertisement, which can double as an order form, specify the time and place the balloons can be picked up or the time and place the balloons will be delivered. Also indicate what will happen if the person designated is not present to receive the balloon(s). One solution for this possibility is for the balloons to be available for the purchaser to pick up.

Similar ideas are balloons with a candy bar attached for Father's Day (perhaps in a church setting) or balloons with a pretty paperweight for Secretary's Day (in a large office complex).

This project is good for a high school or college. Do some research with potential customers if you want to try it in other settings.

Success story: Valentine Balloons and Serenades
Resources: St. Louis Carnival Supply; STUMPS—One Party Place

VALENTINE THEME

A Valentine theme is popular for dinners, dances, and shows close to February 14. Decorations feature items like hearts, Cupids, lace, bows, and flowers; color schemes are usually red and pink or red and white. Programs feature songs, skits and plays about love and couples—famous, ideal, or what to avoid.

VICTORIAN BOOTH

The merchandise for this booth will reflect the highly ornamented style of the period of Queen Victoria. There will be a lot of lace, ruffles, brocade, fancy picture and mirror frames, and old fashioned items such as doilies, runners, cushions, and embroidered pictures. The chairperson of this booth needs to be enthusiastic and knowledgeable about items appropriate for this theme.

Resources: Dover Publications, Inc.; Trafalgar Square Publishing; Victoria; Victorian Decorating & Lifestyle; Victorian Sampler

WATERMELON CUTTING

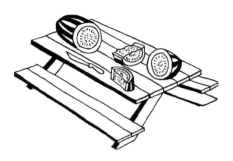

When watermelons are at their best, schedule a watermelon feast, selling either by the piece or on an all-you-can-eat basis. Try to get a good price by buying in bulk. Sell any leftover melons to be taken home. This will probably work best in conjunction with some other meeting, program, or event. Don't forget the salt shakers, and be sure to have knives, forks and spoons available. Prepare for the cleanup being messy. The customers will need a place to wash their hands.

WEEKEND AWAY

Offer a stress-free weekend away from the normal routine. Arrange to pick up the participants at their front doors in a limousine or deluxe bus; provide someone to take care of their luggage. Serve refreshments and provide soft music as they travel. Choose a destination that is off the beaten path and has quiet, pleasant surroundings. Be sure there are fresh flowers, a fruit bowl, quality candy, and current magazines waiting in the rooms. Provide for exceptional meals that require no table hassles, paying or tipping. If possible, secure after-dinner entertainment of the old-fashioned singer and piano type. Begin Sunday morning with wake-up coffee, rolls and the morning paper. Arrange no activities; allow the participants to sleep, read, participate in a nearby church service, or go for a walk as they decide. After brunch, repeat the easy travel routine for the trip home. Be sure to advertise this weekend for what it will be so that only those who desire this type of trip will pay the considerable sum you'll charge for the pampering.

WET SPONGE THROW

Ask individuals such as school administrators or teachers, group leaders and officers, coaches, umpires, policemen, and politicians to serve as targets for wet sponges. If they are brave and have a sense of humor, they can garner funds for the group with very little overhead expense.

You will of course test the sponges and the distance to be sure the strongest and most accurate customer can do no harm. Conduct this event in a location which will not be damaged by being wet for a long period of time.

If this idea appeals to your group, consider having the authority figures agree to have their heads shaved or receive a Mohawk haircut if a set amount of money is donated.

WINDOW WASHING

Offer crews for hire to wash windows inside and out at the same time. Take all needed supplies and equipment to the site. Have enough people in the crews to provide for someone to brace the ladder and hand the washers the items they need. In the advertisement, define what types of windows you will wash. Remember your goal is to raise funds for a good cause and price this service to reflect its strenuous nature. Consider that there is the potential for injury to workers in this project.

Resource: Writer's Digest Books

WOOD PRODUCTS BOOTH

You need workers who will create a variety of wooden products for this booth. Unless the volunteers can donate their work you must consider the profit markup you can expect. Another possibility is to collect secondhand wooden furniture and household items and have workers clean and or refinish them. Products can include shelves, bookcases, vegetable bins, chests, toys, flower stands, picture and plate stands, picture frames and mirror frames.

Resources: Dover Publications, Inc.; Meredith Press Corporation; Rodale Press, Inc.; Sterling Publishing Co., Inc.

YARD BOOTH

Gather things for yards: birdhouses; bird feeders; birdseed; birdbaths; chimes; windsocks; sundials; flower containers; plants of all kinds; yard decorations; porch furniture and decorations; yard swings and furniture; mailboxes; name signs; books and leaflets on growing plants, building patios, etc.; and tools for working in the yard.

Resources: Dover Publications, Inc.; Rodale Press, Inc.

SUCCESS STORIES

The fundraising events featured in this section are operated by volunteers or, in a few instances, by an organization staff member who depends upon volunteers to form the work force. They are all success stories in that they have raised a significant amount of money for their worthy cause.

The individuals featured did not operate the events by themselves; they are the first to insist that raising money is a group activity requiring volunteer workers and customers. The people interviewed for this section are, however, inspirations to all who desire to be successful at fundraising. Without exception, they are dedicated, energetic, and willing to share their expertise with others. They possess impressive talents and know how to enlist others in their cause. In a few instances, the leader who provided information and recommendations requested that only the name of his or her organization be given.

Most of this book is a collection of ideas for fundraising. The purpose of these stories is to illustrate how an idea like any of those featured in the first part of this book is the beginning point for planning an event tailored to the resources and needs of the group needing money. The fundraisers also share valuable information and suggestions for those interested in similar projects to raise funds.

ARTS AND CRAFTS FAIR

The Sappington House Foundation Board is a group of 15 to 20 cooperative and enthusiastic volunteers who plan and support the fundraising efforts of the Sappington House Foundation. One of the organization's annual projects is an arts and crafts fair that has been held the fourth Sunday in September each year for about 18 years. The money earned is used for maintenance of the historical Sappington House.

Planning for the arts and crafts fair is done year round. The chairperson of the fair changes from year to year, but the volunteer group is stable. The information collected regarding operating the fair is available to each year's leader.

A committee inspects the wares of all applicants before they are allowed to reserve a booth. Quality standards are thus maintained, and the organizers believe this policy has contributed to the success of their fair. Monitors also inspect all booths to review the merchandise available; if the quality is below the expected standard in spite of the preview before the show, the exhibitor will not be accepted in future years.

The event is held outside, and those renting booth space provide their own tables, chairs, and display racks. In case of rain, the show is moved across the street to a school. The fair is advertised on the radio, in local newspapers, and through posters and flyers. In addition to the renting of booths to those with arts and crafts to sell, the volunteer group operates a bake sale during the fair. They also earn money by selling coffee and doughnuts to exhibitors during the early morning when they are setting up their booths. After the fair, the volunteers meet and critique the event. Information and recommendations are recorded for the committees to have for reference as they plan for the event the next year.

The most recent annual fairs had about 100 booth operators who paid an average of $20 for one section of the display area. The profit range for the event is $1,800 to $2,400.

Other successful fundraising projects used by the Sappington House Foundation volunteers include a gift shop in the historical house and a quilt show.

AUCTION

Diana Dauphin founded and is the executive director of High Hopes, Inc., a nonprofit corporation which each fall hosts a dinner and silent auction followed by an oral auction. High Hopes uses all funds raised to make it possible for individual students at Central Visual Performing Arts High School—a magnet school in St. Louis—to participate in "experiences which will enrich their talents and lift their ambitions for the future." The organization's goal is to be sure no CVPA student misses an audition, a scholarship interview, or an arts workshop because of lack of funds. Diana and all others associated with High Hopes and the auction are volunteers.

The dinner was held in a quality establishment which was willing to provide facilities and a schedule which accommodated the auction. Tickets were sold at the price needed to provide the dinner and location for the event; all profits were made on the silent and oral auction.

All items for the auction were donated. In addition to items donated by personal contacts of the workers involved, Diana made an energetic and organized effort to obtain donations from celebrities from all walks of life. Letters requesting donations were mailed about six months before the auction. As soon as an item was received for the auction, a form was completed in triplicate, a decision was made as to whether to use the item as a silent or oral auction item, and an item number was assigned. The item was then tagged with the number, a description was entered into the computer database for the program, a thank-you envelope was addressed and filed for use after the auction, and a thank-you letter was prepared, leaving the amount received to be typed in after the auction. All items were stored by category upon receipt. Items for each silent auction table were boxed together in groups of approximately 25 items per table; items for the oral auction were boxed separately. Each box was labeled to indicate content.

The auction was advertised by announcements at meetings, flyers, letters mailed to past and prospective participants, and news releases to local newspapers. Ticket sales were limited to the capacity of the site. Some people who could not attend sent donations and these were gratefully acknowledged.

Auction items were transported to the hotel by van and helpers unloaded them. The silent auction tables were set up, the oral auction items were displayed, and all auction items were tagged with their number. It took about six hours of diligent work to prepare for the event.

The following schedule for the evening was included in the advertisements and with the tickets: 6 P.M., doors open; 6:30, silent tables start to close and bar opens; 8:00, buffet; 8:45, oral auction begins. The closing of the silent auction tables was announced from the podium. Workers supervised the bidding at each table. Items purchased were processed by a committee and the buyers paid for and received the items at the end of the oral auction. The oral auction was conducted by two auctioneers who took turns. The event lasted between five and six hours including registration of guests, the silent auction, the dinner, the oral auction, the payment for purchases and clean-up of the site.

An ice chest filled with donated spirits was offered as a raffle item. Tickets were sold for two months prior to the auction and during the evening of the auction. The winner did not need to be present to win, but the drawing took place near the end of the evening.

At this writing the fifth annual auction had been completed; proceeds that year were approximately $10,000. Diana Dauphin offers the following information and recommendations for others who are considering using an auction for fundraising:

- It is important to be organized in every aspect of the event. One person needs to oversee the details and coordinate the efforts of the workers.
- Many items donated for the silent auction can be grouped together. For example, you can combine certificates for movie rentals with a pizza or fast food coupon, or place together ball game or theater tickets and a donated dinner.
- Limit the oral auction items to a number which can be auctioned in a reasonable length of time. People who are tired do not bid as well as they would normally. The oral auction determines the length of the event, and the goal is to dismiss while everyone is still enjoying the evening.
- Strike a balance between the "personal touch" and the efficiency provided by a computer. High Hopes addresses all envelopes by hand, and personal thank-you notes are written to everyone who helps or participates in the auction. The computer is a valuable tool for producing the form letters (which can be individualized), the program for the evening, advertising flyers, etc.
- Develop a mailing list for requesting items to auction and constantly update it by deleting those who have not responded to several requests for an item and add new names for each auction. Another mailing list is needed for individuals receiving invitations to purchase tickets.
- During the dinner, the person in charge of the fundraiser should visit each table to make sure everyone is enjoying the evening. Diana Dauphin also takes a photograph of every table group and includes a print of the group picture in the thank-you note each person receives; this custom seems to be appreciated.

An auction is time consuming and challenging but can be built into a financially rewarding annual fundraiser. If you plan to raise funds for an extended period of time, consider becoming a fundraising corporation, getting nonprofit status from your state, and applying for federal tax-exempt status. Discuss the advantages and disadvantages of these actions with an attorney and seek professional help in completing the required steps. High Hopes was able to accomplish these goals with the help of free legal advice.

Other successful types of fundraising events which Diana has helped sponsor include coupon book sales and organization cookbook sales.

AVON FUNDRAISER

Susan Morice is an Avon representative who is also an active member of the Mother's Club of St. George's School. She organized a sale of Avon products to benefit the children of the school. Each student took home a copy of Avon's Easter sale book and a cover letter explaining the fundraiser. Orders were also taken at a meeting of the Mother's Club.

Susan and two other volunteers handled the sale. The product is well known and sold well. Orders were received for about three weeks and when the products arrived they were promptly delivered to the purchasers. In most cases the student who obtained the order received the merchandise to deliver.

The school's tax-exempt letter was given to the Avon company and all sales were tax-free. The company was very supportive of the project. The school received 40 percent of the sale price on all items purchased. Susan donated her services. The Avon fundraiser earned $400 to benefit the school.

Susan Morice offers the following advice for others interested in this type of fundraising event:

- The main requirement for this type of sale is the help of an Avon representative. Look for a representative in your group or someone associated with those who will benefit from the money raised.
- The ideal time for a sale of this type is in late November to benefit from Christmas shopping.
- This type of fundraiser is simple and effective and requires only a few workers to be successful. It is important to have potential customers who strongly support your worthy cause.
- If you are raising funds for a group other than a school, all members of the group are potential salespersons.

BAZAAR

The members of the Union Methodist Women's group have a bazaar, collectibles sale, and bake sale each November to support their mission projects. About 30 volunteers plan and implement this event in a team effort. The bazaar features hand-crafted merchandise. The collectibles are items which have more potential value because they are attractive to collectors. A Resell-It table at the bazaar features merchandise contributed for the group's rummage sales. All members of the group contribute goods to the bakery booth. A committee also raises funds with a soup and sandwich lunch.

The event is advertised through flyers in stores, a free ad in the local newspaper, and by word of mouth. The planners always hope for good weather, which is important to the success of the event. A group of dedicated women prepare the craft items all year round. They meet on Monday nights from February to November to work together. Although they purchase some of their materials, many donated items are used. Volunteers prepare a wide variety of items: Christmas tree ornaments, wreaths, basket arrangements, other Christmas decorations, and gift items such as dolls with clothing, men's handmade ties, bookmarks, etc. The crafts committee will fill special orders for customers when they can.

Two members of the women's organization look through the rummage sale donations and set items aside for the Collectibles and Resell-It booths. Examples of the collectibles are old handkerchiefs, gloves, clip-on earrings, necklaces, cups and saucers, and enamel cooking pans. A member of the group who is interested in antique items serves as chairperson in selecting what will be sold in this category. Sometimes the advice of an antique shop owner is obtained. The Resell-It Booth features nearly new items and can include almost anything; however, cooking utensils, dishes and other kitchen items are popular merchandise for this booth. The range of income from the bazaar, collectibles sale, and bake sale is $2,000 to $3,000.

Other successful types of fundraising events used by the Union United Methodist Women include spring and fall rummage sales and a June salad luncheon, book review and mini-bazaar.

BINGO

Norm Schicker is considered the resident expert on bingo by the volunteers who operate the Notre Dame High School bingo fundraisers. The Parent Organization of the high school operates Saturday night bingo all year round. The profits from the bingo games are used to benefit the students of the school. Norm knows all the state and local laws which govern bingo for non-profit organizations. He keeps the necessary records, completes the required forms, and pays the required fees. He usually is one of the 10 to 12 volunteers who work during the Saturday bingo sessions.

The school cafeteria and adjoining hall are used for the bingo games. Patrons pay $14 for admission. To play nine bingo cards costs $15, or more may be purchased. Only cash is accepted—no checks. In the middle of one wall is a console for the caller where numbers are selected and displayed electronically and announced over a public address system. Five television monitors display the numbers called and are placed so that everyone can see one of them. During each game large boards indicate all the numbers which have been called.

Each player receives a one-page program which indicates the way a person can "bingo" on each of 22 games and the amount paid to the winner. The way to win a game ranges from "regular" to "butterfly" to "snowflake." The prize for winning ranges from $100 for a regular game to $500 for an ending coverall. Half of the program page gives 17 rules, such as the following: You must bingo on the last number called; numbers must be clearly marked on paper when called; no other bingo will be honored after caller begins to verify a bingo; no one under 16 years of age is allowed to play bingo or permitted in the hall; etc.

Players are seated at long tables. When a person bingos, a volunteer who serves as a runner gives the winner a flag and takes the card to the caller to be verified. If the card is declared correct, the runner pays the winner in cash.

In addition to bingo, a heavy business is done selling pull tabs for $.25, $.50 or $1.00. The pull tab workers sell and pay winners at any time. A player wins on a pull tab when he or she pulls back one of the five possible tabs and reveals a combination of symbols specified on the back of the card as a winner. Winning combinations have a payoff ranging from $.50 to $500.

The supplies needed to operate a regular bingo game are available from a number of companies. Norm's group purchases items made by Capital Game Manufacturer, Cleveland, Ohio, through a local retailer.

Workers at the bingo game sell daubers (markers designed to place read-through color on numbers as they are called) and food to the players. The average attendance for a bingo night is about 200 patrons. The average profit for the year is $13,000. Norm Schicker offers the following information and advice for others who are considering using bingo for fundraising:

- Be sure you know and follow all laws governing the operation of bingo in your local area and your state.
- His state allows no one under 16 to work or play at a bingo game. They are not allowed to advertise; promotion must be by word of mouth. Investigate carefully so you will be aware of the regulations of this type.
- It takes Schicker about 12 to 15 hours a week to keep the records and make reports for the money earned by his group.
- It is important to have bingo every week in order to build a group of regular players.
- The selling of pull tabs makes more profit than the bingo games.
- Once you are confident you have the customers needed to operate a bingo night, buy the console for the caller, TV monitors, etc. as soon as you can; the equipment will increase your income and pay for itself.

- Use masking tape to attach large garbage sacks to the end of each table to collect trash and to speed clean-up.

BOOK FAIR

Willis Potthoff is a 35-year veteran book fair volunteer. After involvement with other organizations sponsoring book fairs to raise funds, he was the founder of the Carondelet YMCA (Y's) Men's Club Book Fair. The Book Fair has been held during late August for the past 16 years and the proceeds support programs of the YMCA.

Books are collected over a period of four or five months. Intensive publicity—through books-wanted bulletins, news stories, advertising, and word of mouth promotion—is used to encourage the public to donate books. The group accepts all donations with appreciation knowing that some books donated will not be appropriate for resale due to their condition or topic. The Men's Club offers a pickup service for donated books and the YMCA staff accepts books for the group daily. The 23 members of the Y's Men's Club and other community volunteers sort, classify and price all books during regularly scheduled work sessions from April until the fair in August.

In addition to distributing advertising flyers and ads in local newspapers, two neighborhood banks include flyers about the book fair in their regular mailings to their customers. The group makes a special effort to hand out advertising flyers at the other large book fair in the area.

The book fair is held at the YMCA during the period when it is closed for annual clean-up. Many boxes of books must be moved from the group's sorting and storage location near the YMCA building.

The books are arranged at the fair site by category so that customers can readily find the type of book in which they are interested. The group has over thirty categories for their books. The categories include, for example, animals, business, children's literature, classics, computers, cookbooks, crafts and hobbies, diet and fitness, medical and health, mystery, occult, romance, science fiction, and self-help. One section of the fair offers new books which have been donated to the group. Willis Potthoff is in charge of a category he calls "old, rare, special and unusual." He has found that interest in these "special" books can lead to feature articles in publications and thus help advertise the book fair. In recent years the group has offered customers over 100,000 hardbacks, paperbacks, magazines, records, tapes and CDs.

The Y's Men's Club operates its book fair from 5 P.M. on Friday evening until 8 P.M. on the following Wednesday. There is a $4 admission fee on Friday evening only. The majority of hardcover books are priced at $.75 to $1 each. Three for a dollar is the price for most paperbacks. On Wednesday only, the last day of the book fair, the price is "all you can carry for $4."

After the fair, the volunteers must work hard clearing and cleaning the site. They store unsold books they think might sell next year and discard the rest.

Income from the book fair has grown from a gross income of about $2,000 the first year to a little over $19,000 in recent years.

A book fair, Willis Potthoff points out, is not a "glamour" operation. It is labor intensive and the preparation work is done among old and dusty books. The books are heavy and must be handled and moved many times. However, no other fundraising project can compare to a book fair when you consider that little experience is needed, little or no "front" money is required, all labor can be done by anyone, and it is interesting to handle books.

The addition of new workers each year is the secret of continued success for an annual book fair, according to Potthoff. Since the project requires much physical labor, the involvement of young people is essential for the health of the group sponsoring the fair. The camaraderie that is developed over a period of four to five months of intensive activity is good for any organization.

BRUNCH AND SPEAKER

Anne Hizar and other members of the Friends of St. Louis Children's Hospital held a brunch to benefit the projects of the organization. The brunch was held on a Friday in April from 10 A.M. to 1:30 P.M. at the Ritz–Carlton Hotel. After the meal, Alexandra Stoddard was the guest speaker; she autographed her books after the program. Stoddard was selected as the speaker based on a survey of the group's board members and was very well received by the audience.

Prior to the brunch, vendors in attractive booths were located in the reception area of the hotel. The vendors included an antiques booth, a pottery booth, a furniture booth and a lace booth. Guests mingled in the area while enjoying a glass of wine or other beverage. Each vendor paid the group $200 for the booth and kept all proceeds from their sales.

The event was planned by a chairman and six committee chairmen who each recruited workers to assist them. Promotion was done through the Sunday paper social page, radio talk show interviews, and area newspaper announcements. Tickets sold for $30. Over 400 guests attended, and the group had a profit of approximately $5,200.

Anne Hizar thinks this event was successful because it was a new idea (the group previously had a luncheon with a fashion show), the ticket price was reasonable, a classy location was selected, and the committee was efficient and worked well together. She advises others considering a similar event that the speaker should be well publicized and be either reasonably well-known or be speaking on a topic that is currently "hot." She also cautions that details related to a contract with a speaker may require careful thought and attention.

Other fundraising events which have been sponsored by Anne or her organization include a black tie dinner and auction; an event featuring an indoor polo game, barbecue, and country dancing; and a debutante ball.

CANDY SALE

Gail Pence is the office co-op coordinator at Beaumont High School. She used a candy sale to pay for an appreciation dinner for the employers of her students. The sale also provided a gift for each employer. The students and sponsors sold $.50 and $1 candy items for two weeks inside and outside of school. There were 11 in the sales force plus some parents who took candy to their jobs to sell. Gail kept a record sheet for each student who took candy to sell. At the top of the record sheet was a signed agreement that the student would be responsible for either turning in the selling price for the candy checked out or returning the candy in good condition. Each time the student took candy to sell or turned in money or candy, the entry on the record sheet was initialed by the student. The sale of a specific amount of candy was needed to pay for each student's and employer's dinner cost. Engraved trophies were given to the students who sold the most candy—first place, second place, and third place. Staff members helped sell the candy before school and during lunch. The group made a 50 percent profit on all candy sold and earned $800 for the appreciation dinner.

Gail Pence offers the following advice for others who sell candy to raise funds:

- Locate a supplier who will deliver the candy directly to the storage area without charge. It is reasonable to expect to make a 50 percent profit from the sale of candy; try not to settle for less. Watch for additional charges, such as a delivery charge.
- If you are selling in a school, check with the administration regarding your planned candy sale before ordering the candy.
- Keep meticulous records and tight control of the candy supply.

- Be sure everyone selling the candy is dependable. Accept help from other adults who offer.

Other types of fundraising events which Gail recommends for high school students include the following:

- Valentine sales (take orders for and deliver Valentine candy, red silk roses, or helium balloons)
- Photographs in front of backgrounds or with costumes (Valentine's Day, Christmas, Old West, funny hats, etc.)
- Dances—formal, informal, sock hop, various themes
- Sale of popcorn made in a machine, taco chips and cheese or salsa, or soft pretzels (all of which stimulate the sale of cold drinks.)

CAR WASH

Meredith Wiecher, a senior at Brentwood High School, has five years of experience helping with car wash projects to raise money. Last August her volleyball team had an exceptionally successful car wash. The money earned was spent on T-shirts for the players and extra equipment.

The team's coach made arrangements to hold the car wash at a gas station located on a busy corner. The station charged the group $25 for the water and the use of half of its lot. The group washed cars from 9 A.M. to 2 P.M. on a Saturday. There were 15 volleyball players and two adult supervisors in the work force. Tickets were sold before the event for $3 a car and $5 a van; several people who bought a ticket did not bring in their car to be washed.

Prices the day of the sale were $5 for a car and $7 for a van. Two workers stood on corners with signs calling attention to the car wash. The girls washed the cars with mild soap, rinsed them with a hose, and dried them with rags. They did not clean the cars' interiors. The amount of profit earned was approximately $400.

Meredith Wiecher advises others who are considering a car wash as a fundraiser to be sure to hold the car wash at a good location where there is heavy traffic.

A car wash is hard work but lots of fun for the workers.

Other successful fundraising projects in which Meredith has participated include a silent auction, odd jobs for donations, and collecting cans to recycle.

CHRISTMAS CRAFT FAIR

Peggy Kroech was the chairperson for a Christmas craft fair to benefit the St. John the Baptist High School. The craft fair was open from 9 A.M. to 4 P.M. on a Saturday in late November. Over a six month period, three volunteers participated in the planning and decision-making for this event; approximately 35 helped in various ways.

The following means were used to promote and advertise the Fair. An ad was placed in the neighborhood newspaper. The committee placed two or three flyers in every confirmation letter and asked the crafters to place them at their favorite businesses. Flyers advertising the fair were delivered to area craft shops. Wooden signs giving information about the event were placed close to the site where the fair was to be held. Radio and television stations were contacted to see if they would advertise the fair as a public service announcement; if they would, information was sent by mail or fax. All of these methods were free advertising and contributed to the success of the fair.

Volunteers spent about 1 1/2 hours setting up for the event and about 2 hours tearing down and cleaning up. There were 90 booths (measuring 9 ft. by 6 ft.) which were rented for $20; the group earned approximately $1,800 on the booths. An additional $350 was earned by operating a concession stand.

Peggy Kroech offers the following information and recommendations for others interested in sponsoring a Christmas Craft Fair:

- Be sure to pick a good weekend (the Saturday after Thanksgiving seems to be the best). Be organized. Expect the unexpected. Be friendly and go out of your way for crafters and patrons.
- Be prepared for the following potential problems: walk-in crafters, crafters that don't like their space, crafters who decide after they get there that they want electricity, and children running around unsupervised.
- If you have other organizations closely associated with your group, consider offering them booth spaces for half price.

Other successful types of fundraising events which Peggy has helped sponsor include a walk-a-thon and a Fanny Mae caramel apple sale.

DINNER THEATER PRODUCTION

Joseph McKenna, president of the K's Theatrical Korps, is credited by the other participants as being the guiding force for a fundraising event featuring an old-fashioned melodrama combined with a dinner. The dinner-theater production benefited the St. John the Baptist parish complex by providing funds to remodel and refurbish their buildings.

The K's Theatrical Korps performed "Ten Nights in a Barroom," a musical comedy exploring the virtues of temperance. In the musical comedy, the actors overacted to the entertainment of all. The villain sneered at the audience; the hero was—most of the time—extravagantly brave and good; the heroine needed saving; and everyone had fun. The show followed a catered dinner featuring roast beef or baked chicken. Six performances were given on Friday, Saturday, and Sunday nights of consecutive weekends.

The price of tickets was $20 for adults and $15 for seniors, students, and children. Group table discounts were available for adults. The profit range was $8 to $3 per patron. The catered dinner cost $7.50 per person plus the cost of coffee, soda, tea, wine and beer offered as drinks. Other production expenses included royalties, the set, publicity and printing.

Over a planning period of about seven months a group of 12 participated in the overall planning. About 100 volunteers were needed to work in some capacity; the volunteers included a cast of 50, 10 stagehands, technical support personnel for the melodrama, and individuals involved in serving the dinner.

Because the event would contribute to the church building campaign, the parish was active in promoting the show to the church members. The pastor was included in the cast and this boosted attendance. The dinner theater was unique to the area and the melodrama, with audience participation, appealed to all ages. The program was advertised in all local papers, local theatrical publications, numerous bulletins in surrounding parishes, and the parish alumni bulletin. Information was also sent to those on the K's Theatrical Korps mailing list. The publicity crew was very experienced and dedicated.

The profit from the dinner theater production was approximately $3,000. This was the group's first experience with a dinner theater, and McKenna and his group feel that this type of event has the potential of earning more.

Joe McKenna offers the following information and recommendations for others who are considering using a similar dinner-theater production for fundraising:

- In retrospect the dinner theater should have been on Saturday nights only and the Friday nights should have been at the regular show prices of $7 for adults, $4 for seniors and students, and free for those 7 years or younger. The dinner theater was not affordable for

"whole families." The Sunday night shows should have been moved to the afternoon for the "seniors" crowd.
- It was difficult to have the food served promptly.
- The auditorium which accommodated the dinner had terrible acoustical qualities.
- McKenna's theater group had 10 years of production experience and had done over 35 shows. They found this style of theater to be very easy to produce. It can be as complicated or simple as you like and still be a great source of entertainment for the audience.
- The K's Theatrical Korps follows these policies with good success: 1. When they ask for help they are very specific about what is needed and how much time it will take. 2. They believe that many hands make light work and seek to enlist plenty of workers. 3. They make it their business that the volunteers know that they are appreciated no matter how large or small the task. 4. They take great pride in their productions and strive to make all facets of production the very best.
- If you are a new group, contact your local community theater groups for help. They exist to help the community. If you have no community theater group, contact the local parks and recreation department and high school drama groups; they are excellent resources.

Joe's group has had good success with three other types of fundraisers: trivia nights (low overhead, minimum staffing, $1,000 to $2,000 net income); a night at the races (medium overhead, moderate staffing, $1,000 to $2,000 net income); and a variety traveling show (a song and dance show with a loose theme which tours local senior citizen homes; charge $50 to $75 per performance for a 60- to 90-minute show; very low overhead and very rewarding).

FAMILY FASHION SHOW

Marie Elcor has a special interest in working with other members of her church to support their parochial high school. One of her projects was a fall fashion show featuring clothes for men, women and children.

Elcor worked with the management of four different clothing stores to select fashions and enlisted models from the members of her planning group, their families, and friends. The event was held on a Sunday afternoon in October in a large meeting hall in their church's educational building. The time was convenient for the working people involved, and the children who took part were not as tired as they might have been during an evening. The location was convenient and available without charge.

The moderator of the fashion show was a woman who was poised in front of the audience, had a clear speaking voice, and was experienced with fashion shows. Personnel from the stores furnishing the clothing for the show helped write the descriptions of the garments modeled. The moderator was prepared to add humor to the show, especially when "pillow people" periodically appeared in deliberately amusing outfits. Two pianists played background music. The models walked down a foot-high runway through the center of the hall. The audience was seated on both sides of the runway.

Models in a variety of sizes and shapes were enlisted. They visited one of the four participating shops where store personnel helped them select clothing to model. The women and teenage girls modeled three outfits each; the men and children each modeled only one set of garments in the show. The models did not wear any special makeup. There was no rehearsal—only instructions just before the show. Two assistant managers from one of the stores involved came to the show and assisted in preparing the models, organizing the dressing room, and pacing the models during the show.

Light refreshments—cookies, punch and coffee—were served before the show; the refreshments were donated by members of the planning group. The fashion show lasted approximately 40 minutes. At the conclusion of the modeling, gift certificates to the participating stores were given as door prizes. One store donated an additional gift certificate.

Tickets sold for $5 per person and $10 per family. The group earned approximately $750 to benefit their school. About 80 percent of those who attended were members of Marie's church and most of the others were brought by members of the congregation.

The following list indicates the number of workers involved in this fashion show: 18 models; 6 in advertising; 2 selling tickets; 2 handling the music; 1 moderator; 2 managing the door prizes; 4 setting up the hall; 5 sponsoring store personnel; 4 dressing room helpers; 6 serving refreshments. Planning and decision making involved 15 to 20 people.

This was the first fashion show of its type for Marie's group, but they plan to have similar fundraisers in the future. Marie Elcor offers the following information and recommendations for others who are considering using this type of fashion show for fundraising:

- The planning period needed is about three months.
- The following factors most determine the success of the show: enthusiasm of the group in regard to advertising the event and sell-

ing tickets; a pleasant location; having door prizes; a smooth presentation; and the wise selection of models.

- Potential problems are keeping the children involved from being too active and getting men to participate in and attend the show.
- The personal touch is the most effective promotion; give invitations individually. Marie's group gave flyers to individuals prior to church with a personal invitation.
- After the fundraiser, thank all workers and store personnel in writing.

Other successful types of fundraising events which Marie has helped sponsor include skating parties, breakfast served (before church), a booth of arts and crafts at a Christmas bazaar, and a car wash.

FIELD PARTY

Marianne Gleich served as chairperson for a unique event to benefit the Eugene Field House and Toy Museum. The night before the opening of a new exhibit, "Baseball: The National Pastime," Marianne's committee sponsored a group trip to the St. Louis Cardinals–Florida Marlins baseball game. Before the game they hosted a picnic dinner under a tent on the lawn of their corporate neighbor next to the museum. Eugene Field loved baseball and the evening honored the poet and supported the museum in his honor.

Tickets were $12.50 and included a reserved terrace seat at Busch Stadium for the baseball game, the "Field party" with the picnic dinner from 5 to 7 P.M., and a $1 discount off an adult ticket to the exhibit "Baseball: The National Pastime" which was on display at the museum for four months after the party. A drawing awarded five tickets to the Batting Cage party room with all the amenities for the baseball game. The purchase of a ticket to the party provided a chance for the five special seats.

Members of the Eugene Field family came to the party. The poet's admirers enjoyed very much meeting his relatives. A musician, in period costume, played the banjo during the picnic in exchange for two tickets to the baseball game.

Most of the cost of the party was covered by several generous corporate sponsors. Most of the food and drink served, the rent for the tent, and five tickets to the Batting Cage party room were all provided. Representatives of the sponsoring companies participated in the party. Their help was recognized in the museum's newsletter and by a personal thank-you letter. Ten people participated in planning the event and about 30 volunteers worked in some capacity.

Over 300 people attended the Field Party. The museum cleared approximately $1,500 from the event. The organizers feel that they received other benefits which were far more valuable than the monetary profit. Because of the event, some of the participants became members of the museum's supporting organization. The museum became more visible in the community due to the advertisements and newspaper articles. The group was recognized on the billboard during the baseball game and had an on-field introduction. The sponsoring corporations developed stronger ties to the museum and have expressed a desire to have joint events in the future.

Marianne Gleich offers the following advice to others who are considering a fundraising event of this type:

- People are looking for something different and somewhere they can go that is unusual or not always available to them.
- Any event planned for outside needs a backup plan. If it had rained the day of the party, the party would have been moved to a local restaurant which is normally closed on Tuesday, which was the day of the event.
- Ask companies and organizations to help you by donating items you need or by paying for something which is essential for your fundraiser. They can do no worse than say "no" and often will say "yes."
- Reconfirm arrangements and services early the day of the event, if possible.
- Expect to have problems. With no restrooms available at the site, the museum had to rent portable toilets. The day of the event, the group lost access to the grills promised and had to find others. A delivery truck got lost. Expect the most problems the first time you have a new type of fundraiser.
- Establish committees with dependable chairpersons so the work will be distributed and the person in charge will have more time to see that everything is well coordinated.

FLEA MARKET AND AUCTION

Barbara Chambers is a leader in planning and conducting an annual flea market and auction to benefit missionary work supported by the Apostolic Pentecostal Church. The youth department of the church sponsors the project with support from the entire congregation.

Two months before the most recent flea market and auction the committee began collecting items donated for sale by individuals and businesses in the area. The more valuable items were designated for sale at the auction; the bulk of the donations were grouped and priced for sale at the flea market. Chambers, who has over ten years' experience with the flea market, was in charge of organizing the merchandise and pricing. She priced low so the items would sell. A committee of 15 to 20 people helped with preparing the items to be sold. They cleaned everything and checked to see that all mechanical items were in working condition.

The flea market and auction was held the second week in June under a large rented tent which was set up by volunteers on the church parking lot. The flea market was open Friday from 5 to 9 P.M. and Saturday from 9 A.M. to 5 P.M. The auction began at 11 A.M. on Saturday. About 20 workers assembled early Friday morning and worked all day to set up for the sale. Since school was not in session, the youth were available to work with the leaders. Barbara and her husband provided an early dinner for the workers just before the flea market opened. At least 40 volunteers worked in some capacity before and during the event.

The Saturday auction was conducted by a professional auctioneer who donates his services each year. Bidders registered by providing their names, addresses, and driver's license information. Each bidder received a number to use in bidding on items. Cash and personal checks were accepted for payment.

A committee operated a food stand. They sold fresh grilled hamburgers, sodas, chips, snow cones and baked goods. A local business donated all the hamburger buns. Saturday night clean-up followed the event. Leftover flea market items were given to the Salvation Army. The flea market and auction earned about $3,000, with the auction bringing in the largest portion of the money.

Barbara Chambers offers the following recommendations for others who are considering a similar fundraising event:

- To earn a good profit you need quality items donated. A worker should visit businesses in the neighborhood and solicit items from them to sell in the auction. It helps if the person asking for the donation is a regular customer of the business.
- While requesting items from the businesses, see if you can place an advertisement in their window or on their bulletin board and or leave a stack of leaflets about the flea market and auction for customers to take with them.
- In addition to newspaper and radio advertisements and advertising through the local businesses, spend some time placing leaflets on cars in grocery store parking lots.

- One person brought home-made pies for the auction, and another provided home-made lasagna; both sold well. Services can be auctioned, such as a night of babysitting; yard or house work; haircuts from a beauty salon, etc.
- Unfortunately some flea market customers may steal items. To combat this, control the entrance and exit to the merchandise area. Have workers staple the sacks of merchandise sold with the receipt attached. Offer a holding service of bags for those entering the shopping area. Attach a number to each bag "held" and give the owner the same number to use to reclaim the bag.
- Be enthusiastic and cheerful as you work, so the project will be more a source of satisfaction and less a chore. Keep in mind the good which will be accomplished with the funds raised.

Other successful fundraisers sponsored by Barbara and other volunteers to benefit their church projects include a church picnic and walk-a-thon and dinners during church events.

HIKE FOR THE HOMELESS

Tonia Chandler works for the St. Patrick Center, where coordinating fundraising projects like the "Hike for the Homeless" is just one of her many responsibilities. The hike is an annual event which involves about 35 volunteers in the planning. Approximately 150 people work in some capacity to make the event a success. The money raised by the group funds programs which are designed to effect permanent positive change in the lives of homeless people.

The date for the event in late April was set a year in advance. The location was one which was convenient for many of the participants and provided adequate parking. A new two-mile family fun walk was added to the five-mile run and the one-mile run used in previous years. There was a special wheelchair category for the five-mile run. Registration fees were $8 for early entries received prior to the race; the day of the race the entry fee was $10. Children under 12 paid $5. The registration fee was waived with $100 or more in pledges collected and turned in on or before the day of the race. Prepaid pledges were to be brought the day of the race. Other pledges collected by the participants were to be delivered within four weeks.

Runners and walkers were enlisted, and the event was publicized through television spots, radio public service announcements, and lots of flyers distributed throughout the city. Special effort was made to distribute flyers in stores which had merchandise attractive to runners. Letters were sent to members of the local track club. Schools received literature encouraging their students to participate. Information was distributed for use in church bulletins and newsletters. The numerous business and organization sponsors helped with the publicity in various ways.

Commemorative T-shirts and water bottles were given to the first 1,000 entrants. Pledge prizes were given to participants who collected specified amounts of money—beginning with those who collected $50. The pledge prizes, all of which were donated, included passes to an amusement park, a cooler filled with sodas, and watches. Winners in 19 categories received trophies.

Registration began at 7:00; at 8:00 the five-mile and one-mile events were run consecutively, followed by the family fun walk. A picnic was planned for 11 A.M. to 1 P.M.

Police assistance was critical to the preparation for the run, and police officers were present to help as needed. The track was laid out and the competition supervised by an experienced coordinator.

The profit from the event was approximately $24,000. The organizers view the increase in public awareness of the needs of the homeless as an important benefit derived from the project.

Tonia Chandler offers the following information and recommendations for others who are considering using a similar event for fundraising:

- Projects of this type are detail oriented. Check on everything and go back later and check again.
- Be aware that bad weather can require canceling the event. If this happens, try to have the cancellation announced by the media as early as possible. Organizers must stay at the site to deliver promised awards, such as T-shirts, and to collect the prepaid pledges that disappointed participants will want to turn in anyway.
- Publicize as much as possible the sponsors who help with the fundraiser. List their names on all flyers, in advertisements, on a large banner at the event, etc.
- Use all the professional expertise you have available to you. Your cause is worthy, so ask for help to make your event successful.
- Following the event, thank everyone who helped. Immediately identify things you can improve and begin planning for the next year.

Other successful types of fundraising events which Tonia has helped sponsor include the Irish Open, an annual golf tournament; an annual St.

Patrick's Day dinner; a country and western party; Jazzercise "Hop for the Homeless"; and a Mardi Gras party.

HOUSE TOUR

Marianne Powers was chairman of the Holly Hills Improvement Association's Second Annual House Tour. The association used the funds for beautification and betterment projects in their area. Projects included painting a bridge, planting an area in a park, and installing a flagpole at a public site.

A committee set the date for the tour and obtained nominations for houses to be included in the tour. Letters were hand delivered to homeowners by a member of the committee to request that they allow their home to be toured. The letter and the messenger gave information about the tour and invited the homeowners to contact the committee members if they had additional questions. (Marianne considers the toughest part of preparing for a house tour to be convincing people to show their homes.)

The committee sent a confirmation letter to all participating homeowners letting them know that the committee would meet with them about seven weeks before the tour. At the meeting the hosts were told what to expect and asked to think about their needs for tour day—the number of helpers they would need, the number of runners needed to protect their carpets, etc. Members of the house tour committee had all served as hosts for a tour of their own homes, so they were well qualified to advise the group enlisted for this tour. Local florists donated floral arrangements for use in the homes. A local realtor provided a shuttle bus that ran continuously to take those on the tour from house to house.

The tour was from 10 A.M. to 4 P.M. on a Sunday. The committee tried to enlist ten to twelve homes for the tour; nine were actually included. Tickets were $10. Refreshments were offered for sale at two locations, but little income was made from the food booths. The house tour was advertised many ways—through church bulletin boards, store bulletin boards, flyers, etc. The local newspaper did a feature article on the tour the day before it was held. Five members of the organization and three helpers outside of the group did the planning and the decision-making for the house tour. About 25 volunteers helped in some way.

After the tour the workers gathered for a buffet dinner. Each participant received a thank-you and a gift. The group then visited all of the homes which had been on the tour.

The House Tour earned approximately $8,000 and is expected to earn more in future years as the event becomes a tradition.

Marianne Powers offers the following information and advice for others planning house tours:

- Although Powers found the planning for the house tour very stressful, the success of the tour made her feel euphoric. She felt proud that she had done something to showcase her neighborhood and to make it a better place to live.
- Some of the problems that can occur in relation to a house tour are bad weather; the concerns of homeowners on the tour (such as fears that people on the tour might be "casing" their home for a future robbery); participants canceling at the last minute and making it necessary to find a substitute; and customers arriving early for the tour before everyone is ready for them.
- When Marianne's house was on the tour she found it very rewarding because the people were complimentary and pleasant.

MEN'S BEAUTY CONTEST

Joyce Brunner is the site director for the Black River Area Development Corporation's Senior Citizen Center at Pocahontas, Arkansas. She was exceptionally pleased with the men's beauty contest sponsored by her organization to raise funds to support the activities of the center. Men associated with the group entered a contest and were judged on their beauty while dressed in ladies' clothing of their choice. The winner was selected on the basis of votes cast by donating money.

About 20 people participated in the planning and decision-making for the beauty contest; 10 workers were needed in some capacity at the contest. About a month was needed for planning and advertising. The contest was advertised by word of mouth and in the senior citizen newsletter in the local newspaper. The group earned $132.32 from the votes received for the various contestants.

After the contest, the group ran a picture of the participants in the local newspaper. They offered a $10 gift certificate to anyone who could name all the men in the picture. They received many responses but only one which was correct.

All who participated had so much fun that the money was little more than a bonus for the event. This type of project has the potential of raising more money, Brunner noted. One problem was the difficulty in locating wigs for all the contestants. Brunner stressed that it is important that the organizers are enthusiastic.

Other successful fundraising events which Brunner helped sponsor include an ugly Easter hat contest (featuring hats made by contestants), inside yard sales, bake sales, and potluck dinners.

MOCK ELECTION

Ray Soaib was elected honorary mayor of the Soulard neighborhood as part of a mock election sponsored by the Soulard Business Association and the Soulard Beyond 2000 Committee. The money made through the election was used to support the Soulard Neighborhood Crime Patrol. The organization pays off-duty police officers to patrol the Soulard neighborhood five nights a week to prevent crime.

The organizers of the mock election charged $20 for a candidate to be placed on the ballot and votes were $1 each.

Ray was encouraged to run by friends at his favorite hangout, Hennessey's Irish Pub. Hennessey's became his campaign headquarters. At first the group was rather casual about participating in the election, but soon everyone became enthusiastic and decided to try to win. The campaign lasted about five weeks. During that time Ray and his supporters raised money through a series of events. They had several barbecue suppers at his home, including a pig roast. Bratwurst sandwiches were sold at Hennessey's with the profit going to votes. There were some beer and pretzel nights with an admittance charge to benefit the campaign. Raffles were held for items donated by businesses to support the cause. The income from the activities supplemented the cash votes.

This tongue-in-cheek election carried the title of a "Serious Political Spoof." Ray limited his campaign promises to supporting graft and corruption. One of his opponents was a neighborhood dog known to all the residents. All 22 candidates and their supporters were working to earn votes by raising money. They worked hard but had fun.

Votes in the election totaled $6,061; Ray Soaib won the election with approximately $1,700 in votes.

A ceremony was held to declare Ray mayor of Soulard. He was given a stars and stripes top hat and a key to the city. The plan was for the new mayor to have no official duties. In reality he has been quite busy representing the neighborhood. He has been interviewed several times by the media, had a place of honor in the neighborhood parade, and been enlisted to serve on a number of neighborhood committees. He makes his rounds in the neighborhood regularly to visit with residents and goes out of his way to greet visitors who express an interest in meeting him.

This fundraiser was so successful that it will become an annual event. Ray and his supporters were on the campaign trail within months preparing to win again the next year.

Ray Soaib plans to win his next election by becoming more efficient raising funds with such activities as dinners (barbecue of all kinds, spaghetti, etc.) and raffles (giving away prizes such as sets of dinner-for-two coupons to neighborhood restaurants).

QUILT SHOW

A quilt show was planned and implemented by the volunteer group which sponsors projects to benefit the historic Sappington House complex. The quilt show has become an annual event.

This show was an exhibition of old and new quilts, none of which were for sale. The quilts displayed were of all types of construction and size; all were quilted by hand. Quilts from the previous two shows were not used again. There was no fee for exhibiting a quilt and no prize money. Quilt owners provided their quilts so that others might see and appreciate them. A "viewers' choice" winner was selected.

The quilt show was held the last weekend in April at a community center. The quilts were displayed on specially made racks and on long folding tables. The group provided insurance for the quilts, and workers supervised the exhibit.

In addition to charging admission to see the quilts, the group earned income by renting booth space to a small number of businesspeople. A quilt shop, bookstore, and vintage quilt dealer offered merchandise for sale. The volunteer workers operated a tea room offering tea, coffee, cake, cookies, and other donated refreshments to customers. About 500 people came through to see 150 quilts, and the group earned approximately $1,500 for its cause. About 20 workers were involved with the project.

The Sappington Foundation Board offers the following recommendations for others interested in sponsoring a quilt show to raise funds:

- Be sure that the quilts displayed are interesting and of good quality and that they represent a broad variety of styles, sizes, and ages.
- Encourage the individuals attending the show to apply to exhibit their favorite quilt in the next year's show.
- An interview in a local newspaper about the previous year's quilt show is an effective way to advertise the opportunity to display a quilt and to promote attendance at the show.

STRAWBERRY FESTIVAL

G. Dale Norfolk has the responsibility of coordinating a Strawberry Festival which benefits the Missouri Baptist Children's Home. In addition to featuring strawberries, the festival includes craft sales, a quilt auction, entertainment, food and other related special activities.

The Strawberry Festival is held the first Saturday in June from 9 A.M. to 3:30 P.M., and all events are outdoors. The event is promoted through ads in the local newspapers, "spots" on Christian radio stations, and materials sent to churches. The planning for the event takes place all year with intensive work the three months before the festival. About 40 volunteers participate in the planning and decision-making and 300 are needed to work in some capacity.

For the most recent festival, 550 cakes were donated to be served with strawberries and ice cream for $1.50 per serving. Food stands sold bratwurst, hot dogs, hamburgers, chicken salad sandwiches, strawberry pies, chocolate covered strawberries, and other items. There was an auction of quilts and special craft items which were made by volunteers and donated. Smaller craft items were for sale in craft tents.

Before the 82 donated quilts were auctioned, they were judged and received ribbons or trophies in several categories. The judges also declared a quilt the winner of the grand prize and another won an overall award for being the most unique.

Every year various singing groups perform on an adult stage and a youth stage. There is a special area where children can play games, have their face painted, talk to clowns, and otherwise be entertained. There is no charge for the entertainment or special events.

The festival earns from $40,000 to $55,000 to benefit the home each year. About 50 percent of the income is derived from the auction of donated quilts and special craft items. Dale believes the Strawberry Festival is so successful because of the 104-year history of the event, the many volunteers who help, and the desire of the volunteers and patrons to help the children of the home.

G. Dale Norfolk offers the following advice for others desiring to establish a fundraiser of this type:

- It is important to have good planning and effective advertising.
- Have activities of interest for all age groups.
- Enlist more volunteers than you think you need; extra workers are an asset and save many complications.
- With large crowds attending, parking can create problems. Have workers directing traffic.

• Government regulations affect things like how food is prepared and served. The IRS required an appraisal of each of the quilts auctioned; purchasers could deduct as a donation only the amount they paid in excess of the value of the quilt. These are examples of tasks which require attention from the planners and volunteers.

The staff and volunteers of the Missouri Baptist Children's Home also sponsor concerts by well-known Christian musicians as fundraisers.

VALENTINE BALLOONS AND SERENADES

Kim Brown, a junior at Rivertown High School, worked with other class members and their sponsors to sell and deliver Valentine balloons and serenades to raise money.

The group promoted the sale through posters and announcements on the public address system. The committee took orders for the helium Valentine balloons and songs at a table located outside the school cafeteria. In three days they had sold all of the 300 balloons they had purchased for the sale. The customers completed an order form which indicated their first choice of color—red, pink, or white—and the person to receive the balloon(s). The customer's name, home room number, and amount paid were also recorded on the form. If customers wished the person delivering the balloons to serenade the recipient, they checked a song from the list of those offered. A pink card with Valentine decorations was prepared by the purchaser to be attached to the balloons. Most customers signed their name to their cards, but many signed them with things like "Secret Admirer" and "Guess Who?"

The orders were separated according to color and whether or not a song was ordered. A team of students was authorized to be excused from class to deliver the balloons and songs. Members of the school choir practiced their serenades. A staff member picked up the rented helium tank and secured it for use in an empty room.

On Valentine's Day the balloons were inflated and clipped, colored ribbon streamers were attached, and the cards prepared by the purchasers were attached. Those ordered to include a serenade were delivered by the singers and the rest were delivered by a separate group of workers. The deliveries were grouped by floors to save time and the workers' energy. Three adults supervised the preparation and delivery of the orders; about 20 different students helped with sales, preparing the balloons, and deliveries.

The price of each balloon was $1 and each serenade $2. The group earned approximately $350 with the project in a school of 725 students and could have sold at least 30 more balloons on delivery day.

Other successful fundraising projects which have been used at Rivertown High School include a dance featuring a costume contest for Halloween, a car wash, candy sales, student versus faculty ball games, and a talent show.

RESOURCES

(Alphabetically by company name)

In your search for resources, look first for established companies in your own community that offer fundraising programs. Approach local businesses for donations and good prices on materials and merchandise you need. Check libraries and bookstores for books which will provide helpful specialized information. Talk to others who are experienced in helping groups raise money and ask them for recommendations on resources.

The companies listed in this section are not intended to replace local resources. They are provided as possible sources for those who need them. While all are considered to be reputable companies, their listing here is not intended to be an endorsement or a guarantee of good service. Research what they offer carefully—just as you should always do before making any purchases or entering into agreements with a company.

ACE-ACME
13434 Northeast 16th Street
Bellevue, WA 98005
800-325-7888

This company's catalog offers a large selection of prizes suitable for carnival games. They also sell tickets and game equipment and supplies. The telephone number above may be used to request a catalog. The company has branch offices in Bellevue, Washington; St. Louis, Missouri; Los Angeles, California; and Chicago, Illinois.

AMERICAN SCHOOL OF NEEDLEWORK
1455 Linda Vista Drive
San Marcos, CA 92069

Sew Creative Projects by Donna Wilder presents ideas and patterns for a wide range of craft projects ranging from wearables to home decorations.

ANNIE'S ATTIC, INC.
1 Annie Lane, Box 212B
Big Sandy, TX 75755
800-582-6643

This company's advertisement says it has "America's Best-Selling Craft Patterns." Call for a free catalog.

BAKER'S PLAYS
100 Chauncy Street
Boston, MA 02111-1783
617-482-1280

Obtain their catalog by sending $1.50; catalogs are sent automatically to customers. The catalog lists plays, musicals, theater books, makeup, dialect tapes, sound effects, and instruction videos. Also included is a Theater Resource Directory which lists suppliers of theatrical goods and services of many kinds.

BALLANTINE BOOKS
201 E. 50th St.
New York, NY 10022
800-726-0600

The book *Color Me Beautiful* by Carole Jackson presents the basics of determining a person's color season—spring, summer, autumn, or winter. *Color for Men* by Carole Jackson with Kalia Lulow presents a system of dressing for men which uses color to their best advantage.

BANNER BLUE SOFTWARE
P.O. Box 7865
Fremont, CA 94537
510-794-6850

"Biography Maker" for IBM personal computers and compatibles provides assistance in recording family anecdotes or full-blown biographies. The program contains over 5,000 questions on over 70 topics and will customize a list of topics for each person questioned based on facts about them.

BANTAM BOOKS, INC.
666 Fifth Avenue
New York, NY 10103
800-223-6834

The book *Color Wonderful* by Joanne Nicholson & Judy Lewis-Crum instructs readers on how to discover their own best and most flattering colors for clothes and makeup.

BARNES & NOBLE
126 Fifth Avenue
New York, NY 10011
201-767-7079

This company's catalog offers 25 different International Music Festival cassettes including *Greetings from Hawaii* and *Mariachi Music from Mexico*.

CAT FANCY MAGAZINE
P.O. Box 52864
Boulder, CO 80322-2864
303-786-7306

This monthly magazines has, in addition to articles about cats, many advertisements for products which are of interest to cat owners.

CHARTWELL BOOKS
110 Enterprise Ave.
Secaucus, NJ 07034

Making Wreaths by Pamela Westland gives advice on finding and selecting suitable materials for wreaths and ideas for a variety of wreath designs.

CHILTON BOOK COMPANY
Radnor, PA 19089
800-695-1214

The book *Sew Sensational Gifts* by Naomi Baker and Tammy Young offers instructions and illustrations for gifts in the following sections: Gifts for Babies and Children; Gifts for Weddings and Brides; Gifts with a Feminine Flair; Gifts for Men and Boys; Gifts for the Home and Patio; Gifts with Country Charm; Gifts for the Bath and Boudoir; Gifts for People on the Go; and Wrapping It Up.

CONTEMPORARY DRAMA SERVICE
Box 7710-J
Colorado Springs, CO 80933
Order Hotline 1-800-93PLAYS

This company's "Theater, Drama & Speech Resources" catalog includes plays for performers of all ages, children through adults; plays and variety scripts for special occasions; melodramas; musicals for middle grades through adults; patriotic plays; comedy skits and sketches; material for clowns; resources for puppet creation and performances; and various offerings in other categories. The company also has a catalog of Christian drama.

COOKBOOK PUBLISHERS, INC.
10800 Lakeview
P.O. Box 15920
Lenexa, KS 66285-5920
913-492-5900   800-227-7282

This company has been printing personalized cookbooks since 1947. They offer many options for covers and features and attractive financial arrangements.

CRAFTS 'N THINGS
P.O. Box 7519
Red Oak, IA 51591-0519
800-444-0441

This magazine offers designs for projects for the home, to wear, gifts, and items to sell at fundraisers. Craft-related advertisements provide information about other printed information and materials available.

CROWN PUBLISHERS, INC.
201 East 50th Street
New York, NY 10022
800-726-0600

Great Gift Wrapping by Elizabeth Lawrence identifies the various materials and techniques of the gift-wrappers' trade and then provides instructions and illustrations for wrapping gifts for various holidays and special occasions.

DEATH IN DELTA
6646 Tholozan Avenue
St. Louis, MO 63109

Request information about this audience-participation murder mystery and you will receive a description of the characters, an outline of the packet contents, and ordering instructions.

DECIPHER, INC.
P.O. Box 56
Norfolk, VA 23501

This company distributes a number of "How to Host a Murder" kits which are designed for party use. These "murder" parties will illustrate for you how a plot and clues can throw suspicion on all the characters and give interested actors experience in playing a part in a mystery and in giving assigned clues.

THE DMC CORPORATION
10 Port Kearny
South Kearny, NJ 07032

Color cards and samples of threads of many kinds and colors are sold directly to the consumer; the names and addresses of mail order firms who carry the DMC products are supplied with a descriptive brochure and an order blank for the color cards.

DOG FANCY MAGAZINE
P.O. Box 53264
Boulder, CO 80322-3264
303-786-7306

In addition to articles about dogs, this monthly magazine has a wealth of advertisements which provide leads on a broad assortment of products of interest to dog owners.

DOVER PUBLICATIONS, INC.
31 East 2nd Street
Mineola, NY 11501

Over 600 books, most priced $3 to $8, are offered in the Dover Crafts and Hobbies Catalog. Titles include: *Old-Fashioned Floral Iron-On Transfer Patterns; Mexican Indian Folk Designs; Easy-to-Do Magic Tricks for Children; Suncatchers Stained Glass Pattern Book; Big Book of Stuffed Toy and Doll Making; Build Your Own Inexpensive Dollhouse; Early American Cut & Use Stencils; Country Design Cut & Use Stencils; Victorian Cut & Use Stencils; Victorian Color Vignettes and Illustrations for Artists and Craftsmen; Victorian Floral Iron-On Transfer Patterns; Decorative Napkin Folding for Beginners; Baby Bears, Bunnies and Other Little Critters Iron-On Transfer Patterns; Russian Cookbook; The Food and Drink of Mexico; Favorite Swedish Recipes;* twelve books related to herbs and spices; three books on magic for children and other selections of card tricks and magic tricks; seven pages of specialized woodworking how-to books, including *Carving Country Characters, Carving Popular Birds, Craving Decorative Duck Decoys, Attractive and Easy-to-Build Wood Projects, Easy-to-Make Bird Feeders for Woodworkers, Making Wooden Toys,* and *Wooden Puzzle Toys;* and general crafts books such as *Old-Fashioned Ribbon Art, Hand Puppets, Easy-to-Make Old-Fashioned Toys, Easy-to-Make Candles, Dried Flowers,* and *Early American Decorating Techniques.* Telephone and credit card orders are not accepted.

ELDRIDGE PUBLISHING COMPANY
P.O. Box 1595
Venice, FL 34284
1-800-HI-STAGE

The Eldridge Plays & Musicals catalog offers scripts in the following categories: Full-Length Plays, Children's Theater, One-Act Plays, Full-length Musicals, Musicals for Younger Actors, Christmas Plays, Christmas Musicals, Skits and Collections. The company also offers an Eldridge's Religious Plays catalog.

ENSLOW PUBLISHERS, INC.
Bloy St. & Ramsey Ave.
Box 777
Hillside, NJ 07205
800-398-2504

Fortune Telling by Carl R. Green and William R. Sanford is written for young people. Its simple style makes easy reading about several methods of fortune telling. The chapter on palm reading in particular offers inspiration for a would-be fortune-teller.

THE EVERTON PUBLISHERS, INC.
P.O. Box 368
Logan, UT 84323-0368
800-443-6325

The magazine *Everton's Genealogical Helper* is published six times a year. In addition to articles pertaining to genealogy, the periodical includes advertisements pertaining to genealogy and reviews of new genealogical books.

FASHION ACADEMY
2850 Mesa Verde Drive East
Costa Mesa, CA 92626

Your New Image—Through Color and Line is a book written by Gerrie Pinckney and Marge Swenson. The book has a section on determining an individual's best personal color palette as well as other topics related to personal appearance.

THE H.W. WILSON COMPANY
950 University Avenue
Bronx, NY 10452
800-367-6770

This company's catalog offers the following books: *When the Lights Go Out—Twenty Scary Tales to Tell* by Margaret Read MacDonald; *Twenty Tellable Tales—Audience Participation for the Beginning Storyteller* by Margaret Read MacDonald; *Fantastic Theater— Make Literature and Folklore Come to Life with Puppet Shows* by Judy Sierra (one section is "Thirty Plays from Around the World"; another is "Hands-on Guide to Shadow and Rod Puppetry"); and *The Flannel Board Storytelling Book* by Judy Sierra (36 programs with poems, songs and stories from around the world, flannel board patterns, audience participation techniques, and follow-up activities).

LEISURE ARTS
P.O. Box 5595
Little Rock, AR 72215
800-643-8030

The leaflet *Bow Making Made Easy* by Patti Sowers gives step-by-step instructions for mastering the art of bow tying.

LONESTAR TECHNOLOGIES, LTD.
920 South Oyster Bay Road
Hicksville, NY 11801-3512
1-800-695-SING

The company sells several models of Singalodeon brand stereo machines with micro-phones which allow singing with taped music. The machines can also be used as portable public address systems. Tapes with instrumental music and voice on one side and music only on the other are available for a wide variety of songs. Some models and specially encoded tapes allow video hookup to a television and the viewing of lyrics on the screen. The company will supply the names of major retailers who han-dle their machines as well as sell most models direct.

McCALL PATTERN CO.
11 Penn Plaza
New York, NY 10001

McCall's has two series of booklets with instructions and patterns for a wide variety of craft projects. Check where McCall patterns are sold or write for information about the booklets "McCall's Creates" and "McCall's Makes It Easy."

McFARLAND & COMPANY, INC., PUBLISHERS
Box 611
Jefferson, NC 28640
910-246-4460

This publisher sells primarily to libraries; if the books listed below are not in your local library, inquire about ordering from the publisher. *Entertaining Children* by Janell Amos; *The Recreation Handbook* by Robert Loeffelbein; *Best Games* by Jennings, Lamp and Stenberg; *Super Treasury of 300+ Activities, Games, Arts and Crafts* by Gayle Vin-yard; *Your Memoirs: Collecting Them for Fun and Posterity* by Seymour Rothman.

MALLARD PRESS
666 Fifth Avenue
New York, NY 10103

Family Circle Country Crafts contains both elementary and advanced projects inspired by nature and the four seasons. It includes projects for quilting, embroidery, cross stitch, doll making, woodworking, rug hooking, knitting and crocheting

MEREDITH PRESS CORPORATION
150 East 52nd Street
New York, NY 10022
800-678-2665

Country Woodworking by Mary Jane Favorite and Nick Engler features about 35 easy-to-make accent pieces, such as furniture, toys, and accessories.

Crafts for Kids—80 Totally Excellent Projects, The Vanessa-Ann Collection contains attractive illustrations and concise instructions for projects for children. Some items include patterns.

MERIWETHER PUBLISHING LTD., PUBLISHER
P.O. Box 7710
Colorado Springs, CO 80933
800-937-5297

Clown Act Omnibus by Wes McVicar says it offers everything a person needs to know about clowning and has over 200 clown stunts to help with entertainment material. *Clown Skits for Everyone* by Happy Jack Feder presents 32 skits for one or two clowns. The skits include prop instructions and performing tips.

MIDWEST BINGO
1124 North 3rd Street
St. Louis, MO 63102
800-422-2775

A catalog with a variety of products related to bingo will be sent on request.

MUSIC DISPATCH
960 East Eleventh Street
Winona, MN 55987

Ask for information about the Decade Series, which includes a separate book of 40 to 60 top songs for each decade of the 1890s to the 1980s. All come in a version for piano, vocal and guitar and a version indicated to be E-Z Play.

NOBLE POPCORN
P.O. Box 157
Sac City, IA 50583
800-537-9554

This company handles a complete line of popcorn products including unpopped popcorn, microwave, and flavored pre-popped popcorn. Their main business is fundraising and the bulk of their business has been focused on the flavored popcorn market. The one gallon plastic canisters for popcorn can be customized through their in-house silkscreening department.

NTC PUBLISHING GROUP
4255 West Touhy Avenue
Lincolnwood, IL 60646-1975
800-323-4900

A "Christmas in…" series of books includes *Christmas in France; Christmas in Mexico; Christmas in Italy; Christmas in Russia; Christmas in Spain;* and *Christmas in Germany.*

Each book includes Christmas traditions, traditional recipes, Christmas carols with scores; and crafts projects related to the country.

OUTLET BOOK COMPANY, INC.
40 Engelhard Avenue
Avenel, NJ 07001
800-733-3000

International Great Meals in Minutes (published by Wing Books) presents meal plans based on food related to 14 different ethnic groups.

PACK-O-FUN
P.O. Box 5034
Des Plaines, IL 60017-5034

This is a family crafts and activities bimonthly magazine. Regular features include "Group Ideas—Crafts for Youth Groups, Schools, Churches and Seniors" and "Storybook Crafts—A Children's Story, with Craft Activities."

PICCADILLY BOOKS
P.O. Box 25203
Colorado Springs, CO 80936
719-548-1844

Creative Clowning by Bruce Fife includes illustrations of three types of clown makeup, examples of classic clown gags, a chapter on balloon sculpturing (creating balloon animals), a chapter on funny juggling, and a chapter on how to be a birthday party clown.

PLAYS, INC., PUBLISHERS
120 Boylston Street
Boston, MA 02116-4615
617-423-3157

Offers one-act plays for young people (lower and middle grades, junior and senior high); a book, *101 Costumes for All Ages*; books on making and operating puppets; and a book of plays for young puppeteers.

PRENTICE HALL GENERAL REFERENCE
15 Columbus Circle
New York, NY 10023
800-223-2348

Max Maven's Book of Fortunetelling by Max Maven is a guide to the varied arts of fortunetelling. This book makes heavy reading, but the following sections could be helpful to a recreational fortune teller at a fundraising event: the two-dice system; the three-dice system; the advanced three-dice system; domino cleromancy; palmistry; and tasseography (interpreting patterns of tea leaves).

RODALE PRESS INC.
Book Readers' Service
33 East Minor Street
Emmaus, PA 18098
800-527-8200

The Weekend Woodworker—Quick and Easy Country Projects has instructions and illustrations for making tables, garden projects, cabinets and chests, children's furniture and toys.

ST. LOUIS CARNIVAL SUPPLY
3928 S. Broadway
St. Louis, MO 63118-4695
314-772-6250

The company offers a huge variety of merchandise at wholesale prices. No catalog is available, but they will send brochures of special promotions and information about specific types of merchandise upon request. They sell imprinted helium-quality balloons, assortments of toys appropriate for carnival prizes, skill games, Hawaiian luau decorations; sombreros & serapes; hats of many kinds, tiaras, crowns; raffle drums for drawings; rolls of tickets; grease paints and makeup; award ribbons; and numerous similar items.

SMITHMARK PUBLISHERS INC.
16 East 32nd Street
New York, NY 10016
800-645-9990

The Magic of Herbs by Jane Newdick has over 100 ideas for using 40 featured herbs. *Perfect Preserves* by M. Dalton King features easy recipes for delicious jams, jellies, pickles and relishes. *The Essential Flower Arranger* by Pamela Westland presents basic principles of flower arranging with easy-to-follow instructions and step-by-step photography for 40 flower arrangements. *Country Fair Food and Crafts* has over 100 things to make for fundraisers, fairs and special gifts.

SPECIAL MUSIC COMPANY AND PAIR RECORDS
560 Sylvan Ave.
Englewood Cliffs, NJ 07632

This company distributes a recording called *Haunted House* which includes such sounds as laughing gremlins, witches and ghosts, chains rattling, a squeaky door, flying bats, etc. *Night in the Graveyard*, the other part of the recording, has sounds of wind, thunder, creaking trees, werewolves howling, ghouls groaning, etc.

STERLING PUBLISHING CO., INC.
387 Park Avenue South
New York, NY 10016
800-367-9692

Nature Crafts for Kids—50 Fantastic Things to Make with Mother Nature's Help by Gwen Diehn and Terry Krautwurst offers illustrated instructions for some appealing crafts projects for children. *Decorating Baskets* by Dawn Cusick presents over 100 baskets to make for gifts and home. *101 Weekend Gift Projects from Wood* by James A. Jacobson has step-by-step instructions and over 200 drawings, photographs and patterns for gifts made from wood. *Wreath Making Basics* by Dawn Cusick has detailed beginner's instructions for creating wreaths and over 80 wreath ideas. *The Decoupage Book* by Holly Boswell has more than 60 decorative projects using simple techniques. *Cross-Stitch: A Beautiful Gift* by Sharon Perna gives instructions and illustrations for seven gifts for Christmas, five Valentine's Day gifts, seven baby gifts and over twenty other gift ideas.

STUMPS—ONE PARTY PLACE
South Whitley, IN 46787-0305
800-348-5084

This company's catalog features an array of products to support Halloween, country and western, and Hawaiian themes, as well as a number of prom/dance themes. There is a wide variety of materials for decorating and a number of kits which would provide interesting backdrops for pictures. There is a collection of luminarias which come with the candle and you supply the sand. The catalog also offers hats, tiaras, crowns, scepters, and royal robes.

SUNSET PUBLISHING CORPORATION
80 Willow Rd.
Menlo Park, CA 94025
800-227-7346

Beautiful Things to Make for Baby features over fifty knitting, sewing, crocheting, and embroidery projects with a materials list and color photos.

TRAFALGAR SQUARE PUBLISHING
P.O. Box 257
North Pomfret, VT 05053
800-423-4525

Victorian Crafts, which was edited by Tracy Marsh, presents over forty projects to make from the Victorian era.

VICTORIA
P.O. Box 7148
Red Oak, IA 51591-2148

Victoria is a monthly magazine containing articles, illustrations and advertisements of interest to those interested in the Victorian style.

VICTORIAN DECORATING & LIFESTYLE
P.O. Box 508
Mount Morris, IL 61054-7995

This is a bimonthly magazine written for those interested in the Victorian style. In addition to the articles and pictures in each issue of the magazine, advertisements will provide leads to sources of crafts and materials and decorations in the Victorian category.

VICTORIAN SAMPLER
Subscription Department
P.O. Box 344
Mt. Morris, IL 61054-7614

Readers of this bimonthly publication receive information and inspiration for projects related to the Victorian style.

WOODBINE HOUSE
5615 Fishers Lane
Rockville, MD 20852
800-843-7323

The book *The Catalog of Catalogs III—The Complete Mail-Order Directory* by Edward L. Palder lists more than 12,000 catalogs organized by subject areas. This would be a good investment for the person who lives in an area with limited access to shopping or who likes to buy by mail order. Some of the listings are specialized catalogs for goods not available in most stores.

WORKBASKET MAGAZINE
P.O. Box 7505
Red Oak, IA 51591-0505

This magazine, which is published bimonthly, has instructions and patterns for a broad variety of needlework projects. Advertisements offer related books and crafts materials and patterns.

WRITER'S DIGEST BOOKS
1507 Dana Avenue
Cincinnati, OH 45207
800-289-0963

The best seller books *Is There Life After Housework?* by Don Aslett has a chapter (9) titled "Don't Be Caught Streaking Windows" which instructs on how to do a professional job washing windows.

INDEX